proclamation 2

Aids for Interpreting the Lessons of the Church Year

pentecost 1

David L. Tiede
and
Aidan Kavanagh, O.S.B.

series a

editors: Elizabeth Achtemeier · Gerhard Krodel · Charles P. Price

FORTRESS PRESS   **PHILADELPHIA**

COPYRIGHT © 1981 BY FORTRESS PRESS

Library of Congress Cataloging in Publication Data (Revised)

Main entry under title:

Proclamation 2.

Consists of 24 volumes in 3 series designated A, B, and C which correspond to the cycles of the three-year lectionary plus 4 volumes covering the lesser festivals. Each series contains 8 basic volumes with the following titles: Advent-Christmas, Epiphany, Lent, Holy Week, Easter, Pentecost 1, Pentecost 2, and Pentecost 3.
CONTENTS: [etc.]—Series C: [1] Fuller, R. H. Advent-Christmas. [2] Pervo, R. I. and Carl III, W. J. Epiphany.—Thulin, R. L. et al. The lesser festivals. 4 v.
1. Bible—Homiletical use. 2. Bible—Liturgical lessons, English.
[BS534.5.P76]   251   79-7377
ISBN 0–8006–4079–9 (ser. C, v. 1)

8564J80   Printed in the United States of America   1–4096

Contents

Editor's Foreword

Proclamation 2: Aids for Interpreting the Lessons of the Church Year offers exegetical comments and homiletical insights to preachers who are committed to treating biblical texts not as pre-texts for rhetoric, but as a challenge to articulate their message anew so that the texts speak across the intervening centuries into our own day. Hence the following pages do not contain sermons, but aids for constructing them.

Pentecost (meaning the "fiftieth") is the Greek name for the Feast of Weeks, which in Judaism prior to A.D. 70 came fifty days after the first day of the Passover (cf. Lev. 23:15ff.). In the OT as well as in Judaism prior to A.D. 70, Pentecost was a harvest festival. Later, because of its association with the Passover, Pentecost was celebrated in commemoration of the giving of the law on Mount Sinai.

According to Luke, the Holy Spirit descended upon the disciples in Jerusalem at Pentecost (Acts 2:1–4). In contrast to Luke, the fourth evangelist narrated that the Holy Spirit was received by the disciples on Easter evening, together with their commission and their authority to forgive and retain sins. The church year follows the Lucan time scheme but retains in its lectionary the Johannine account. Both evangelists insist that the Holy Spirit is God's eschatological gift and power which are inseparable from Jesus, his life, passion, and resurrection (Acts 2:33; John 20:20–24). Thus Pentecost celebrates the presence of Jesus during the time of his absence.

It should also be noted that while the Gospel of cycle A is the Gospel of Matthew, we have no suitable text in the First Gospel that deals with the coming of the Holy Spirit upon the church. Hence the presence of the Johannine account of the Day of Pentecost, cycle A. Matthew repeated the tradition that Jesus will "baptize you with the Holy Spirit" (Matt. 3:11 // Mark 1:8), but he did not develop this tradition, probably because at his time Christian enthusiasts separated their claims of inspiration from the words and works of Jesus.

The Sunday following Pentecost is observed as the festival of the Holy Trinity. Christians have not said all that is meant by the word

God until they have spoken about God the Father and Creator, Jesus his Son our Lord, and the Holy Spirit who puts the spotlight on the Father and the Son and inspires us to faith, love, and hope, and unites us with all believers in the one holy catholic church. The custom of assigning this day to the celebration of the Holy Trinity originated in northern Europe during the Middle Ages and became official procedure by order of Pope John XXII in 1343.

Whereas Lutherans and Anglicans identified the following Sundays as Sundays "after Trinity," the Roman Catholics (with the exception of the early rites of the Dominican order) and the Orthodox churches called these Sundays "after Pentecost." This is certainly preferable and is followed in the new lectionaries.

The Second Lessons for the Second Sunday after Pentecost to the ninth are selections from Rom. 3:21 to 8:27. These lessons are frequently placed in striking and illuminating tension to sections from Matt. 7:15 to 13:30. Both Second Lessons and Gospels indicate what Christian existence, with its promises, resources, and challenges, is all about.

The exegetical parts of this volume were written by David L. Tiede, Professor of New Testament at Luther Seminary, St. Paul, Minnesota, and author of *The Charismatic Figure as Miracle Worker* and *Prophecy and History in Luke–Acts.*

The homiletical sections were written by Aidan Kavanagh, O.S.B., Professor of Liturgics at Yale Divinity School and author of *The Shape of Baptism: The Rite of Christian Initiation* and *The Canon Revisions of Thomas Cranmer, Archbishop of Canterbury.*

Gettysburg, Pa.   GERHARD KRODEL

Homiletical Preface

For their own protection, readers should know at the outset where this homiletician stands. What follows is a series of presumptions that will be at work behind the homiletical interpretations of the lessons listed in this volume and so well exegeted by my colleague, Dr. Tiede.

Above all, the Jesus of the readings is Messiah, the Christ—the Promised One, the Anointed Lord of creation and of church. Not only his teaching but his very self are given to the community of those who believe and strive to live in him. His teaching and his self together constitute the good news, the gospel, which both summons and serves the church to assemble for worship of the Father, through the Son, in the Holy Spirit. In this sense, the public ministry of the Anointed One not only continues, it also fills and overflows the church met for worship, spreading from there out into the world and setting the missionary and ministerial purposes for which the church exists in him.

This gospel is enunciated differently in each of the ten sets of readings. But it remains nonetheless one gospel heard and obeyed by one people. This people, this assembly of faithful ones, always hears the gospel fresh but never for the first time. It lives by this gospel, feeding constantly on it for necessary nourishment. Such a gospel therefore must never be dismembered or trivialized. The preaching of such a gospel in such an assembly is a worshipful event carried out not by analysis of texts but by images marshaled in direct ratio to the nature and spirit of the assembly's worship taken whole. The liturgy is the ceremonial of the Word, and the Word has been made flesh.

The homily or sermon, being one part of the worship event, intends not so much to instruct the hearer as to leave the whole assembly in a condition to pray. The homiletical task is not to communicate the unknown to the unknowing but to rally the knowing about the known in their midst. The homily or sermon rises out of the shared sacramentality of the Word made flesh.

To accomplish this, the preacher must be steeped in the sacred text, in the worship tradition of the particular assembly, and in the actual pastoral condition of the assembly to which the preacher ministers. The preacher's craft must therefore be of a high order. But the marks of the chisel must never show, attract attention, distract, or over-power, lest virtuosity mutate into condescension. The preacher's peculiar ministry is simply to speak the gospel clearly and reverently, serving both him whose it is and those who are his.

The homiletical interpretations which follow are not meant to be preached, because they are not written for congregations. They are written as meditations on the sacred texts for the use of preachers setting out to prepare what they will say to congregations whose abilities and needs they know far better than I possibly can. My only hope is that these interpretations will not do an injustice to the gospel or to those whose duty is to preach it clean and unalloyed.

New Haven, Conn.   Aidan Kavanagh, O.S.B.

The Day of Pentecost

Lutheran	Roman Catholic	Episcopal	Pres/UCC/Chr	Meth/COCU
Joel 2:28–29	Acts 2:1–11	Acts 2:1–11 or Ezek. 11:17–20	1 Cor. 12:4–13	Joel 2:28–32
Acts 2:1–21	1 Cor. 12:3b–7, 12–13	1 Cor. 12:4–13 or Acts 2:1–11	Acts 2:1–13	Acts 2:1–21
John 20:19–23	John 20:19–23	John 20:19–23 or John 14:8–17	John 14:15–26	John 20:19–23

EXEGESIS

Disciplined historical exegesis may be particularly salutary when one is interpreting such familiar texts as those appointed for the Day of Pentecost. Each of the passages reflects a specific life situation in which earlier authoritative traditions have been resignified for the believing community. Thus the modern interpreter or proclaimer need not be restricted to extracting words and phrases from these passages in order to speak of the work of the Holy Spirit in a liturgical setting. Rather, the scriptural writers themselves set a precedent for the application of more ancient oracles and stories to new occasions.

First Lesson: Joel 2:28–29. This passage must be seen within the literary whole of the book. The force of its promises and eschatological vision is best estimated by its contrast with the grim specter of the locust plague and drought announced in the opening verses (1:1–2, 11). Only returning to the Lord and God's gracious repentance (2:12–17) has turned his vengeance into the vindication and blessing of his people (2:18–27). The awesome prophetic vision of the great and terrible day of the Lord is of apocalyptic and cosmic proportions, but it is still tied to the historical assurance of the preservation of the nation and holy Zion from destruction.

The exact historical occasion of the entire book escapes precise determination, but most scholars would locate it in connection with a particular crisis in the early postexilic Persian era (ca. 500 B.C.). The constant cultic references and frequent allusions to the fate of Zion point to a strong association with the temple as the locus of rituals of repentance leading to a renewal of divine assurances.

The content of such assurances is highly traditional. Ezekiel 33—39 also constitutes a summation of the authoritative traditional promise of the "restoration of the fortunes of Jacob" (see Joel 3:1) and the pouring out of the Spirit of the Lord upon the house of Israel (Ezek. 39:29; Joel 2:28). Here Joel proclaims the approach of the fulfillment of such promises. "All humanity" (or "flesh") envisions all Israel becoming a nation of prophets, just as Moses' word in Num. 11:29 had also suggested.

The pouring out of God's Spirit means the people are empowered. Saved from the impending destruction (2:30–32), the survivors shall be a restored and vindicated people. The day will come when all will live in intimate communion with God, and God's reign from Zion will be established.

Second Lesson: Acts 2:1–21. The spectacular events of Pentecost are identified in Acts as the fulfillment of the Joel prophecy. Ascribing the fulfillment of this prophecy to "the last days," Acts marks the descent of the Spirit as the manifestation of the promised reign of God's Spirit through the agency of the exalted Lord and Messiah Jesus (2:32–36). This use of scriptural prophecies is strikingly similar to the *pesher* exegesis at Qumran: *pishro,* "this means" the eschatological fulfillment has taken place (see 2:16).

Faithful Israel has been reconstituted around the chosen twelve and all the devout Jews and proselytes. A new era of repentance in preparation for the day of the Lord has been inaugurated for Israel.

The manifestations of the Holy Spirit are depicted so as to gather a host of scriptural images of the descent of the Spirit upon Israel (see Num. 11:25–27) and to document John's promise of a baptism with the Holy Spirit and fire (Luke 3:16). Whether the inspired disciples speak in coherent languages or dialects (vv. 4, 8) or in ecstatic utterance so that the miracle is one of hearing (vv. 8, 13), the question "What does this mean?" (v. 12) moves the reader to the scriptural exposition. Peter's proclamation (vv. 14–36) enriches the interpretation of Joel 2 with a messianic argument from Psalm 16 in order to specify the fulfilled promise that requires Israel's repentance (2:39; Joel 2:32).

According to Acts, those in Israel who heard and received this proclamation displayed the faith of reconstituted Israel by repentance and Baptism. While other stories in Acts will deal with the rejection of Christian preaching by many in Israel, this passage is one of several that emphasizes that thousands in Israel received the message in repentance unto salvation. Restored Israel will yet realize its glorious vocation of being a light to the Gentiles (Luke 2:32; Acts 13:17; Isa. 42:6; 49:6). This assurance must have been all the more startling to the reader of Acts if Jerusalem had already been sacked by Rome and if the question "Lord, will you at this time restore the kingdom to Israel?" had become a plea.

Gospel: John 20:19–23. The Fourth Gospel presents yet another vision of the empowerment of the disciples by the Spirit. Harmonizations of this account with that of Acts may obscure the distinctive emphasis of each. This resurrection appearance, however, shares many traditional features with that of Luke 24:36–47, especially as later scribes adjusted Luke's text. The repetitions of the greeting "Peace be unto you" (vv. 19, 21) and the transition phrase "When he had said this" (vv. 20, 22) have further stimulated diverse attempts to reconstruct the sources and traditions used by both evangelists.

In its final literary composition, John's brief passage contains a miraculous appearance of the resurrected Lord (vv. 19–20), a sending of the disciples (v. 21), the giving of the Holy Spirit (v. 22), and the bestowal of the authority to forgive or retain sin (v. 22). All of these elements are integrally related to John's specific understanding of the Spirit's work in the community. The identity of Jesus as the one sent from and in complete unity with the Father is fundamental to the Fourth Gospel. It is this Jesus who is recognized and who has the authority to deputize his disciples (17:1–26, especially v. 18). His giving of the Holy Spirit is therefore a transmission of divine power and authority. The authority to forgive and retain sins thus becomes the distinctive mark of the church's bold claim to exercise this divine prerogative. The scandal of this claim was obvious to all of the evangelists (see Mark 2:7 // Luke 5:21 (23:47) // Matt. 9:3 (16:19;

18:18). John's account thus reflects a succinct statement of exactly how this authority of the Holy Spirit was transmitted to the church.

HOMILETICAL INTERPRETATION

A generally unremarked advantage of beginning each Sunday's sequence of readings with an OT lesson is that it helps the worshiping assembly to perceive something of how God's self-disclosure progresses like a slow and stately dance in the midst of human affairs. This perception is an initial lesson in the way God deals with humankind. It helps to qualify the notion suggested by our self-centered urgency that God's patience is impassive to our needs, like the fixed stare on the face of a primitive statue. In response to our pleas for immediate and total deliverance—from oppression, from the intractabilities of creation, from sin, from ourselves—he seems only to abide.

The divine clock does not tick in synchrony with ours. In fact, it does not tick at all, but hums without waver the unbeginning and unending constancy of existence which is God himself. We often attempt to reduce the unqualified existence of the Creator to a human scale. The quality of life we insert between the ticks is history. And here it is that the unending divine dance reduces us to its rhythms; here God's self-disclosure advances according to his pleasure and our own true needs; here we discover ourselves to be stepping to Another's tune as we execute a dance we thought we ourselves had designed. Our crowded square dance imperceptibly modulates into a cosmic pas de deux.

Today's three readings each witness, at different times and from distinct perspectives, stages in this modulation process. All three seem to be marshaled on this day in order to give common if not identical response to the question, What is the end of the community's faith? To determine what this common response is and to present it with integrity are the preacher's task. It is a task that cannot be accomplished by exegesis of texts alone. It must proceed by first realizing that God's word is a living Word present still in the community assembled now on this day.

Pentecost Sunday is not merely a random time at which a congregation commemorates the historical circumstance of the Holy Spirit's first outpouring upon those of faith in Jesus. The Day of Pentecost did not even begin as a Christian feast. For Jews it marked no historic event but brought Passover, the great feast of Israel's chosen-nationhood, to a finale of a week of weeks and Sabbaths plus one eschatological "eighth day," the first day of the aeon that lies beyond time, the fiftieth day, Pentecost. This was the observance in which, according to Acts, the little community was engaged when all that Passover and Pentecost had meant to them as Jews was suddenly and disconcertingly fulfilled. The consummation of all things rushed in upon them, catapulting them into the "eighth day" of creation restored by the Creator-Word's day of labor on the cross and his Sabbath of rest in the tomb.

It is crucial that today's preacher understand that the community in which he or she preaches is this same community. The day is the same; the Creator-Word is the same; the consummation of all things, the Holy Spirit, is the same. The obvious differences in the number of the year and in geographic locale are precisely the differences which make no difference. God's sovereign will abides; its effects on those of faith abide. Both preacher and community stand on holy ground.

The holy ground of this day, say the lessons, is rooted in Easter as the pouring out of the Holy Spirit is rooted in the resurrection of the Lord, as the faithful Christian's Spirit-graced vocation of witness is rooted in the Christian's conversion of repentance and Baptism. Nor is the latter merely an appropriation of the former. The Christian's baptismal vocation is rather the concrete way in which the Lord's resurrection and sending of the Spirit still works its presence and effects in the world. What he has become he bestows upon the church in each of its members.

What the members become in him by baptismal conversion and baptismal living necessarily shows forth for all others to see (1) the beginning of the eschaton, (2) the reconstitution of faithful Israel, (3) and the fullest possible revelation of the Messiah as God in Christ (Acts). This is no novelty. It is but the consummation of the divine pleasure already recounted and prophesied in the depths of the OT (Joel).

In this sweeping perspective, the end of the community's faith is not nostalgia for a beloved Master who represented long ago, but briefly, the world's most shining hour. Rather, the end of the community's faith is nothing less than a life deep in the heart of a restored universe, a witness to the radical newness of all things as they proceed therefrom. Such a community is a spirited people, the dimensions of whose life in faith will be the subject of the lessons for the next nine Sundays.

The Holy Trinity
The First Sunday after Pentecost

Lutheran	Roman Catholic	Episcopal	Pres/UCC/Chr	Meth/COCU
Gen. 1:1—2:3 or Deut. 4:32–34, 39–40	Exod. 34:4–6, 8–9	Gen. 1:1—2:3	Ezek. 37:1–4	Gen. 1:1—2:3
2 Cor. 13:11–14	2 Cor. 13:11–13	2 Cor. 13:(5–10) 11–14	2 Cor. 13:5–13	2 Cor. 13:5–14
Matt. 28:16–20	John 3:16–18	Matt. 28:16–20	Matt. 28:16–20	Matt. 28:16–20

EXEGESIS

First Lesson: Gen. 1:1—2:3. The creation account of Genesis 1 is generally assigned to the Priestly strand of Pentateuchal traditions and dated in the exilic era. Its profound sense of cosmic and cultic order is probably best understood as a theological testimony to an age when such coherence was far from obvious to Israel. Perhaps God had forsaken his people or was impotent in the face of the overwhelming powers of chaos and destruction. Perhaps the Babylonian astrologers were correct, that human destiny was under the capricious sway of the movements of the heavenly bodies. Perhaps the cosmogonic forces of the wind and seas and powers of the deep had to be appeased. Perhaps humanity must resign itself in submission to these powers. Perhaps even the bearing of children in such a world works only to perpetuate bondage to this malevolent order.

No element of this account is casual. From the creation of order out of waste and void *(tohu wabohohu)* to God's benediction of goodness on all of creation and the divine sabbath rest (1:31—2:3), every feature displays the sovereignty of God over fearsome and awesome forces and powers that were potentially full of mythological significance. In God's good time and through God's beneficent and purposeful activity, all was ordered, placed, and named. God's assignment of all of the earth and its plants and animals to human dominion is thus not an invitation to exploitation. It is an assurance of God's continuing concern for human welfare through the gracious bestowal of permission and authority to manage fields, flocks, and institutions. Even the sevenfold ordering of time reflects the Priestly author's conviction of God's good intention for all of creation.

The fascination that this passage had for later Gnostic interpreters is also noteworthy evidence of its radical affirmations. In the era of the NT and early church, disdain for the world as a "corpse" and a "tomb" entrapping the human soul evoked many heretical and spiritualized attacks on creation as the work of a deceitful demiurge. But the straightforward testimony of Genesis 1—2 to the goodness of God's purposes in creation and care for the cosmos and humanity resisted all rigid dualisms.

Second Lesson: 2 Cor. 13:5–14. This passage is so full of traditional phrases that it may be tempting simply to mine it for the Trinitarian language of the last verse. But the timeliness of that liturgical language should be marked much more precisely by reference to the serious difficulties and churchly altercations that have been discussed in the previous chapters.

Chaps. 10—13 appear to stand as an identifiable unit, perhaps even as a separate fragment of Paul's Corinthian correspondence. At any rate, he has attained new heights and depths of irony and sarcasm, polemic and pathos in his appeal for the integrity of his apostolic ministry. Having suffered from the comparison with the prowess of the "superlative apostles" (12:11), he has resorted to ironic and foolish boasting and finally a thinly veiled threat concerning his impending arrival (13:10). Thus the concluding imperatives are not merely general moralistic maxims: "Mend your ways, heed my appeal, agree with one another, live in peace." Those are the pastoral commands of the apostle whose entire vocation has been under attack.

The benediction therefore also has a particular force. To be sure it may already be traditional, but it corroborates the message that Paul has been defending. The gentle grace of the Lord Jesus, as disclosed in the weakness of his crucifixion, provides the final assurance to a community that is too readily impressed with power and perform-ance. But it is this grace that reflects and conveys the love of God, producing the common bond in and through the agency of the Spirit.

Gospel: Matt. 28:16–20. This passage constitutes Matthew's dis-tinctive presentation of Jesus' transmission of authority and mission charge to the church. It can be compared profitably with last Sunday's text from John. Matthew's presentation of Jesus as having taught with authority (7:29), healed with authority (8:9), and forgiven with author-ity (9:6, 8) culminates in his being given "all authority in heaven and on earth." Jesus, Messiah and King of the Jews, has been exalted to dominion over the world, exercising that authority in part through his disciples until the consummation of the age.

Matthew's version of the commissioning of the church is reminis-cent of the charge attributed to the "men of the Great Synagogue" in rabbinic tradition. "These said three things: Be deliberate in judging, and raise up many disciples, and make a hedge for the Torah" ('Abot 1:1; see also 'Abot 1:12 and Matt. 23:15). Yet the emphasis on making disciples of all the nations (Gentiles) must not be missed. Not only has Jesus previously empowered the church to act on behalf of God and God's Messiah in forgiving and retaining sins (16:18–20; 18:18–20), but now the Messiah's mission to Israel is expanded to all the nations.

While both John and Luke-Acts have also used similar stories to interpret the *departure* of Jesus, Matthew stresses that this episode reveals the continuing *presence* of the exalted Messiah. Having pre-viously identified Jesus as Emmanuel (1:23) and having emphasized the assurance of his continuing presence and intercession among his disciples (18:19–20), Matthew also depicts Jesus' final words to the community in the same light. The church does not "go it alone" or possess its own authority. Its mission and mandate continue to be derived from the abiding presence of its Lord, to whom all authority has been given.

HOMILETICAL INTERPRETATION

Last Sunday's lessons dealt with the object of the community's faith. This Sunday's lessons deal with the scope of that same faith.

Significantly, the First Lesson is the Genesis account of creation. It is the story of the world's foundation as a free act of God's own brimming existence. It denies that creation is merely a random jumble of abutting forces without meaning or the capricious act of some cynical demiurge with no purpose other than to entrap all that exists in the fatality of matter.

To misunderstand the story as being about the how or when of creation is to miss the fact that it is really about the nature of creation viewed in the light of creation's why. The radical affirmation of the Genesis story is that not out of need but out of the sheer abundance of his being God brought into existence conditions which both support and nurture a being made in his own image and likeness. Since the Original is a community of Persons, the image and likeness must also be a "communion-being." Male and female God made them, abounding in charitable fertility so that these two might share their individual existence with offspring who would in turn be made in the same image and likeness. Humankind was to be a community of persons presiding at the center of a free and meaning-laden order of sustained reciprocity between the whole of creation and its divine source.

So basic for Christian faith is this creation-wide scope that the earliest church lectionaries place the Genesis reading first among all the lessons to be read at the great vigil of Easter, when Baptisms occurred. In such a context, Baptism was seen to involve far more than an individual's subjectivity. Rather, Baptism was viewed as the definitive entry into that new creation which was consummated in the work of Christ, who restores all things in himself. The Creator-Word became Redeemer-Word, perfecting the creation which humankind had flawed by disobedience and restoring communion with creation's abiding source.

Into nothing less than this does the baptized enter. Nothing less than this does the continuing presence of Christ among his faithful people celebrate. As such, he himself is the living paradigm of the ecclesial style this faithful people gives to a restored world. The mode of Christ's presence, says Paul in the Second Lesson, consists not in power or in virtuosity of performance but in weakness and gentleness made strong only by dwelling in truth. This is the way the reborn are to live in a reborn world whose source and whole preoccupation is communion in Father, Son, and Holy Spirit.

Given this scope to Christian faith, however, there is no motive for complacency. For the very nature of communion in God thrusts outward. As the Trinity's communal existence thrusts outward into creation and recreation in Christ, so those who live in him cannot avoid being swept up in that same thrust which created and redeemed all things.

That those who have been graced with life in the Father by Christ, and who thus live in the Spirit, should not be sent forth to share this life with others is an impossibility. As Son and Spirit proceed from the Father, as Messiah comes forth from Israel to all nations, so too must a faithful people emerge from its radical communion in the source of all to share that life with all. Matthew's account of Jesus' commission to the disciples of his own authority and his command to make disciples of all nations does not, in this sense, add any new formality to the nature of the church. It only specifies, in terms that cannot be missed, the outward thrust which is wholly intrinsic to the communion in God which a faithful people sustains by grace and effort.

All this makes inescapable the fact that a church which exhibits no symptoms of evangelism, a church to which missionary endeavor does not come with a certain natural ease in a sustained manner, is a church at least verging on apostasy from the communion which begot and nurtures the world. The radical affirmations of Genesis, Paul, and Matthew require the scope of Christian faith to encompass the whole sweep of God's creation as well as Christ's saving recreation. There is no attic in which a church can hide from these truths, for the attic is found also to be the handiwork of that community of Persons which holds all things in being.

This Trinitarian view of things is radically communitarian and cosmological in scope. It is also profoundly biblical, the work of Jesus Christ lacing it with evangelical and missionary specifications. Christian theology at its best has reflected on the premier NT ordinances or sacraments, Baptism and Eucharist, against this backdrop. Baptism incorporates one into a faithful community which consummates its fellowship with all things around the Lord's table by giving thanks to the Father through Christ in the Holy Spirit. The two hinges upon which the "sacramentality" of God's creation and redemption swing are Baptism and eucharistic Holy Communion. Far from separate events at the outer edge of Christian life, Baptism is the way Eucharist begins, and Eucharist is the way baptismal conversion and initiation are sustained in the church's life of evangelical and missionary existence. Baptism and Eucharist together call us home to that Trinitarian community which is the source of all. Baptism and Eucharist at the same time impel us outward to serve that sublime source as bearers of its free and gratuitous love for all.

The scope of the community's faith is Trinitarian and cosmological in itself, evangelical and missionary in outward thrust, and thus baptismal and eucharistic in practice.

The Second Sunday after Pentecost

Lutheran	Roman Catholic	Episcopal	Pres/UCC/Chr	Meth/COCU
Deut. 11:18–21, 26–28	Deut. 11:18, 26–28	Deut. 11:18–21, 26–28	Deut. 11:18–21	Deut. 11:18–21, 26–28
Rom. 3:21–25a, 27–28	Rom. 3:21–25a, 28	Rom. 3:21–25a, 28	Rom. 3:21–28	Rom. 3:21–28
Matt. 7:(15–20) 21–29	Matt. 7:21–27	Matt. 7:21–27	Matt. 7:21–29	Matt. 7:15–29

EXEGESIS

First Lesson: Deut. 11:18–21, 26–28. These excerpts from Deuteronomy 11 are best understood as hortatory applications of the curse (vv. 16–17) and blessing (vv. 22–25) which are crucial features of the "declaration of basic principle" made to Israel in this section (10:12—11:32). The literary device of the recitation of authoritative Mosaic traditions leads to this remarkable summation of Israel's peculiar obligations and privileges before God. Ostensibly directed to the people on the verge of their entry into the land by the departing

Moses, this section appears particularly appropriate as an appeal for reform in a later era when actual options of national policy and identity are being entertained.

The problem of "serving other gods" (vv. 16, 28) was both a result of the influence of the nation's powerful neighbors and a reflection of the persistent strength of local religious customs. The forcefulness of the appeals to be faithful to the ordinances suggests a heightened sense of urgency. The very fate of the nation is at stake, but not on account of some external threat or doubt of divine faithfulness. Rather the continued possession of the promised land depends upon the observance of "all this commandment which I command you to do, loving the Lord your God, walking in all his ways, and cleaving to him" (v. 22).

Each person in the nation is confronted with personal responsibility. Diverse techniques are to be devised to ensure that all the people be constantly confronted with the commands, and a national educational policy is to be mobilized to assure that each new generation understands. As in the time of Josiah's reform, which is the most likely date of the material (2 Kings 22—23), this appeal precludes any presumption on God's promises. The clearly stated curses for nonobservance apply not only to matters of national policy but also to individual practice. Every person and family must be held accountable for faithfulness to the commands, on which the continued blessings of God's promises depend.

Second Lesson: Rom. 3:21–28. As the previous passage from Deuteronomy shows, Israel with good reason had long understood its faithful observance of the Torah to be requisite to its salvation. The righteousness of God was disclosed in the Torah, compelling and inviting a repentant people to discover the source of its health, national prosperity, and eschatological assurance. But what happens when the Jewish messianist Paul includes non-Jews in his preaching? What is the effect of his declaration that "now the righteousness of God has been manifested apart from law, although the law and the prophets bear witness to it"?

Paul's Letter is not quibbling with a trivial legalism or preoccupied with the psychological difficulties of an overzealous conscience. It is making a theological claim that since Christ, the sine qua non of salvation, even Israel's eschatological assurance is no longer observance of the Torah but trust in what God has accomplished through Jesus Christ. The priority of God's active righteousness is as uncompromising as his Torah had ever been. Even to depend upon faithfulness in Torah observance and the traditional rituals of atonement is to cut oneself off from God's dramatic and dynamic righteousness proffered to humanity in Jesus Christ. Those Christians who place their trust in Jesus and yet invoke all the ancient commands for Israel's special observance as conditions of salvation fail to grasp the dramatic consequences of this active intervention of God and his righteousness. They threaten to diminish the atonement which God's righteousness has required and supplied in Jesus' death, reducing it to a supplementary satisfaction.

There is no middle ground. The old faithfulness has become a distrust of God's decisive act if it is somehow required of all believers. Paul's theocentric vision discloses the will and plan of God, who deploys his righteousness, justifies the ungodly, and expiates the sin of all gratuitously, finally to prove and display his righteousness to an unbelieving world. God's independence of his holy covenant with Israel does not imply its denigration. Indeed the Scriptures attest to God's faithfulness to that covenant. But once surpassed by his decisively gracious display of righteousness in Christ, relying upon Torah observance and the sacrificial cultus of Israel for salvation implies a fatal lack of trust in divine righteousness and faithfulness shown forth as grace in Jesus Christ. That trust, that passive righteousness of the Christian before God's justifying initiative, has now supplanted active Torah observance as the assurance of salvation.

Gospel: Matt. 7:15–29. Matthew's presentation of Jesus' Sermon on the Mount concludes with these awesome words. The differences in sequence and content between Matthew and Luke caution against hasty conclusions concerning details in their common source and its redaction, but in Matthew the resounding command for faithfulness to this teaching in *word and deed* constitutes an appropriate and compelling ending of the sermon. Vv. 28–29 thus serve as an explicit redactional summary, highlighting the astonishment of the crowds at the authority of Jesus' teaching.

Indeed the power and uncompromising demand of this Jesus may be both astonishing and demoralizing for many readers, ancient and modern. The messianic license that Jesus has taken with the interpretation of the law has only made its demands more stringent, while stripping away a host of accommodating traditional interpretations that made the observance of the law more attainable as a way of life. Not even those who profess their faith, prophesy, exorcise, and perform mighty acts in Jesus' name were assured of eschatological favor from this Jesus. While the commands of Deuteronomy appeared resolute but promising, and the righteousness of God in Paul offered a divinely initiated salvation, Matthew's Jesus becomes the issue himself.

The Messiah-Teacher Jesus exercises great freedom in his interpretation of the law and his healing and demands a decision about his person and role. For those attempting to hedge their religious bets while evading the radical demands of this Jesus, his teachings expose their pious assertions as hypocrisy. But for those whose hearing and trusting of Jesus' authority lead to unguarded obedience, all the promises of the reign of God through his Messiah are already assured.

HOMILETICAL INTERPRETATION

If last Sunday spread out the scope of Christian faith, the readings for this Sunday insist on the interior quality of that faith.

The three lessons each stress that there is something unyielding about that quality. Not only is it nonnegotiable, it is as unavoidable as a volcanic eruption, and its results are just as irresistible. This applies to the quality of the faith as well as to its contents, for both quality and contents are rooted in the implacable will of God even as they unfold dynamically and by stages in human history. It cannot be forgotten that Jewish and Christian faith is covenant faith, and that while the covenant is bilateral, the parties to the agreement are as unequal as creation is to its Creator. Any parity we may claim with the Other Party to the contract is by the sheer grace of the Other; it arises not from any merit of our own. The covenant provides no motive for a prideful human faith. On the contrary, human sin broke the aboriginal communion of our race with God, making necessary a new relationship which God's merciful justice established as law.

About this the Deuteronomist leaves Israel in no doubt at all. The nation is to immerse itself in the law to which every citizen, young and old alike, will be held accountable on pain of national "death." It is not an easy law meant only for external observance: it is to be engraved on hearts and minds, to be taught to children at their mothers' knees, to be the subject of domestic discourse, the subject of prayer on retiring and rising. It conditions Israel's very survival for the future, for without the nation's relationship with God established as law Israel is nothing.

Although the law was a grace of God for Israel, it cannot be forgotten that God's fundamental grace was a new relationship with him for the whole of a fallen race. A sin that was worldwide elicited a new communion by grace with God for all. Of this Israel was curator and chosen repository. Better, Israel was the womb in which the seeds of grace would grow through the evolutionary stages of law and ultimately into the consummation of all things in One who emerged from the very loins of Israel itself.

On this both Paul and Matthew agree. Jesus' concluding words to his great sermon astonished his hearers then, and in all probability they will astonish the assembly today, for they are radical in the extreme. He does nothing less than gather the whole of the law into himself, declaring in effect *la loi c'est moi.* Thus for Paul, the new Deuteronomist, Jesus the Christ, not the law, is the sine qua non of salvation. Jesus, the Messiah of God, is the issue. The community's faith is adamantly Christic.

When one reaches this point, a certain tendency to provide quick ethical solutions often takes over. Many preachers may wish to speak of the Christ-centered quality of the community's faith in terms of following or imitating Christ in daily life, of the need to become Christlike in daily living. While there are some grounds for going this way to be found in the lessons themselves (less perhaps in Romans than in the First Lesson and Gospel), it is a way that is easily sentimentalized, especially by preachers who feel more comfortable with ethical applications than with doctrine. The trouble is that ethics may end by controlling doctrine rather than doctrine controlling ethics. Should the two reverse or float apart from each other, then as often as not the preacher's own unexamined assumptions, personal problems with faith, or subjective guilt feelings may imperceptibly take over— from a gospel-founded doctrine of the Christ—as ethical criteria for Christian living. When this happens, the scope of Christian faith is constricted, and the end of that same faith is misplaced. A Christianity of ethical solutions is in danger then of becoming an endeavor in works-righteousness, its content little more than a potpourri of messages whose proof is found not in God's serene will but in whether or not it helps to think positively and to live successfully according to obscure standards.

Paradox, irony, and fidelity to the gospel as traditionally received in the church are together the only way to subvert this reductionist tendency, which is subtle in its imperceptibility. Hard as it may be for some to hear, the Christ of Christian faith ascended not ladders of political power but mountains to pray, a cross on which to redeem a fallen world. He was less a religious educator than an exorcist of the darkness infesting human hearts and minds which no amount of education can penetrate. He never asked his followers to think for themselves but to invest total trust and unguarded obedience in himself, even to failure and death on a cross. He summoned people not to the observance of natural law but led them through it to the divine law of which the natural is only the jumbled manifestation on this side of time and space. He came not to cure us of our ills but to free us from death itself. He eased no human tension but intensified those tensions which really matter, and to an incandescent degree. He taught that life was to be had only by throwing it away freely and that a slave could be more free than his master. He healed the world by tearing out its guts and calling it the kingdom. And then in his bloody hands he bore us home.

The Third Sunday after Pentecost

Lutheran	Roman Catholic	Episcopal	Pres/UCC/Chr	Meth/COCU
Hos. 5:15—6:6	Hos. 6:3b–6	Hos. 5:15—6:6	Hos. 6:1–6	Hos. 5:15—6:6
Rom. 4:18–25	Rom. 4:18–25	Rom. 4:13–18	Rom. 4:13–25	Rom. 4:13–25
Matt. 9:9–13	Matt. 9:9–13	Matt. 9:9–13	Matt. 9:9–13	Matt. 9:9–13

EXEGESIS

First Lesson: Hos. 5:15—6:6. The prophet is gifted and burdened with the pathos of God caught up in an intense struggle with his defiant people. The fury, the ardor, the hope, and the despair of God are astonishingly anthropomorphic and anthropopathic. Platitudes concerning the love of God are swiftly overwhelmed by Isaiah's prophetic vision of divine passion, as intense in its hatred of unfaithfulness as it is preoccupied with the hope of repentance and restoration through forgiveness.

The historical setting for these oracles may well be the oppression that followed the conclusion of the Syro-Ephraimite war by Tiglath-pileser III's conquest (733 B.C.; see 2 Kings 15:27–30). The apparent calm is founded on tribute paid to Assyria by an illegitimate king. Instead of healing its wounds, God will rip them open (5:13–14). When the cult returns to its pious prayers and assurances of God's favor, the prophet's word will cut them down.

In superb prophetic irony, the hypocrisy of all of Israel is confronted and exposed. The people say that God is as faithful as rain, but they are as fleeting as mist. They say God's help is as sure as the dawn, but it is God's judgment that flashes forth as the light. The bitter truth is that none of the superficial rhetoric or ritualism has come to terms with the depth of God's frustrated anger toward their unfaithfulness. The knowledge of God so confidently invoked (6:3) is profound in its requirement of much more than perfunctory observance (6:6). The same intensity of God's passion for his people that is reflected in divine anguish ("What shall I do with you, O Ephraim? What shall I do with you, O Judah?") produces a scathing denunciation and threat against complacency. Until the people of God understand and plumb the depth of his steadfast love, their corrupt political alliances and ceremonial rituals will only evoke his harsh judgment.

Second Lesson: Rom. 4:13–25. Abraham's faithfulness was commonly understood to be his peculiar virtue. The Book of Genesis and a broad spectrum of Jewish traditions recorded Abraham's persistence in trusting and obeying God when the external evidence was all but nonexistent. The one-hundred-year-old man whose body was as good as dead and whose wife was dried up continued to be a source of amazement and delight to all of his offspring. But was Abraham exemplary in the first instance because of his unswerving reliance upon God or because of his continual faithfulness to God's law? For many of Paul's Jewish contemporaries, including many Christians, it was exactly Abraham's diligent observance of the law that constituted his faithfulness and required all of his descendants to practice circumcision and ritual observance.

Paul's argument must not be regarded as an antinomian or even an anti-Torah polemic. In fact he emphasizes the upholding of the law by this faith (3:31). But the case that Paul is constructing is specific to his concern for the inclusion of the Gentiles as Gentiles (for example, without circumcision or ritual observance) on the ground of their saving trust, and this argument rests on two pillars. (1) Even for Abraham and all his physical offspring, God's promise was granted as fully efficacious solely on the basis of that trust, with obedience to the law simply following as the sign or seal that was required of Israel. But that faithfulness of ritual observance was secondary in sequence and significance. (2) Appointed as the "father of many nations," Abraham's patrimony was therefore not limited to his physical descendants who faithfully preserved the sign of circumcision, that is, the nation of Israel. No, all who shared Abraham's implicit trust in God's promises, and specifically those Jews and Gentiles whose trust enabled their recognition of Jesus as the fulfillment of the promises, all those believers were to be reckoned as descendants of Abraham. To reverse the sequence and make obedience to the law requisite for all for the granting of God's promises is to misconstrue both God's faithfulness to Israel and his proffering of justification through Jesus to all those in the "nations" "who share the faith of Abraham, for he is the father of us all" (v. 16).

Gospel: Matt. 9:9–13. This section of Matthew features Jesus in a series of episodes where he is confronted by requests and challenges from diverse quarters (8:2, leper; 8:5, centurion; 8:14, Peter's mother-in-law; 8:19, a scribe; 8:25, his disciples; 8:28, two demoniacs; 9:2, a paralytic; 9:3, some of the scribes; 9:11, Pharisees; 9:14, disciples of John; 9:18, a ruler; 9:20, a woman; 9:27, two blind men; 9:32, a demoniac). The circumstances are briefly described in each vignette, but the net effect is the presentation of a series of difficult cases which test Jesus' authority as a teacher and his power.

The calling of Matthew (9:9) is related with such economy that it serves simply as a telling illustration and introduction to the objection of Jesus' close fellowship with tax collectors and sinners. The scribal charge of blasphemy (9:3) and the complaint of John's disciples concerning Jesus' lack of asceticism surround this episode and heighten the interest in the specific case. While the Pharisees had made a policy of the separation of the godly from those who were careless about observance of the law and complicit with the heathen imperial armies, Jesus' table fellowship suggested that God's eschatological wedding feast would be thrown open to the most unlikely assemblage (Matt. 8:11–12; 9:15).

To establish Jesus' role as teacher and to represent this as a case of authoritative scriptural interpretation, Matthew supplements Mark's account with Jesus' title as "teacher" (9:11), portrays his charge to the Pharisees as rabbinic instruction ("go and learn," 9:12), and grounds the traditional maxim concerning the sick needing a physician on the scriptural warrant "I desire mercy and not sacrifice" (9:13). The entire episode thus becomes a Christian midrash on Hos. 6:6, demonstrating the precise force of that word in the new context of the messianic age. Much more than a complaint about external observance, this passage provides the church with a startling disclosure of the will and plan of God and a definitive interpretation of the prophetic tradition in the mission of the Messiah and his disciples. The very religious scruples that would produce a self-justifying and insular religious community are divulged as hypocrisy by the unveiling of the scope and method of God's saving purpose. Either this Jesus is the Messiah and teacher of Israel or he is a subverter of the faith.

HOMILETICAL INTERPRETATION

Given the end, scope, and quality of the community's faith, today's lessons place before the assembly three "icons" of its faith's nature, that is, of its principle of operation. The nature of the faith is constituted by those aspects of its being which give most immediate rise to the way it acts.

The first icon of this is of two spouses locked together in a tempestuous marriage. Hosea pictures God as a husband whose love for his wife is anything but the romantic platitude of two people awash in a sea of good feelings about themselves and their relationship. The husband's love is fierce and exclusive; the wife's is easygoing and tends to wander. She is ritually obsessive about keeping the kitchen clean. God's anguished and exasperated passion for his espoused people is not reciprocated. His love is like a steady rain, theirs like a light mist that vanishes at dawn, inconstant. Until they learn to accept the passion of God's love on its own terms, their relativizing liaisons and obsessions will evoke only domestic strife. Israel must come to terms with the fact that it is yoked not with an indulgent sugar daddy but with a vigorous and jealous mate whose exclusivity is rendered the more intense in view of the messianic issue of their union. Their marriage is as painful to both as it is urgent toward an end that lies in the future. It is a wedding not of convenience but of necessity, and like all such unions it is difficult. Romantics need not apply.

The second icon touching the nature of Christian faith is of one serene figure, Abraham, who looks very much like Jesus himself. Paul sees Abraham, patriarch of Israel, in a posture of calm and unswerving fidelity to the law as it is rooted deeply in the unwavering divine will not only for Israel but for all nations. Unlike the inconstant spouse in Hosea's vision, Abraham abides in God's design for the world, swerving not at all; accepting, obeying, and rising, not without anguish at times, to every demand that comes his way for the as yet dimly seen ends of the divine purpose. It is in this that Abraham seems at times to become the image of Jesus himself. And to the sharp eye, this latter image begins to look like the vast multitude of all those, Jew and Gentile alike, whose steady fidelity to God's promise enables them to discern its glorious fulfillment in Christ, God's anointed Messiah. The subtle dynamism of Paul's sweeping theological icon of the nature of the community's faith is breathtaking.

But no less so than Matthew's sharply etched image of Jesus in the flesh, teaching with both confident power and stunning authority, disposing of a series of hard cases while being charged with blasphemy, a lack of asceticism, and consorting with sinners like Matthew himself. Unrattled, Jesus avoids no question. He settles them authoritatively and cuts behind their captious intent, leaving the questioners with more truth than they perhaps cared to have. The icon Matthew gives us is a powerful image of Jesus who, because he takes on all comers and dines with all, will require his followers to do no less. They will have to eschew insularity, obsession over observances, and self-justification. For them nothing can be foreign save sin; nor will the world be able to restrain or contain them, since it was unable to restrain or contain him. His table and theirs is the world; the food upon it is food the world cannot give. The feast they celebrate is both the funeral repast for a dead world and the birthday party of a world made new. There is no middle ground here for reasonable negotiation, for he who sits at the table's head is either Messiah of God and consummator of time or subverter of faith. Those who sit around the table, moreover, are either the hope of the world or of all those in the world the ones most to be pitied. Their faith in God in Christ, like Abraham's, mirrors God's fidelity to Israel and the world, or it mirrors nothing at all.

In sum, the three biblical icons contained in today's readings make clear that the nature of the community's faith is threefold. First, it is eschatologically catholic; that is, consummate, whole, total, and meant for all (Matthew). Second, it is unswervingly trustful of God's gracious pleasure in Christ (Romans). Third, it is fiercely passionate in its loving response to the love which first begot the world and then redeemed it from its sin, restoring the world to communion with its divine source by espousing it to him whom it nonetheless slew even as it lay in his embrace. This third aspect is an image so astonishing in its scandalous profundity that not even Hosea would have been so rash as to have suggested it; nor could Paul, in his extension of the marriage metaphor, had he remained ignorant of Christ's passion and death.

One trouble with these three aspects of the nature of faith is that each of them is easily caricatured, even by the well-meaning. To say that a community's faith is eschatologically catholic is sometimes taken to mean that it should be bereft of standards and should forgo critical judgment. To say that this faith is unswervingly trustful of God may be construed to mean that the community should set out to save itself while losing its own soul. To say that this faith is fiercely passionate may give rise to Torquemadas, Mathers, and Savonarolas.

Such caricatures are risks which Christian faith, as displayed in today's scriptural icons, has to take. But the risk involved in not taking them is greater still. For the faith cannot forgo being eschatologically catholic and survive as a sectarianism of the present moment, becoming a Church of What's Happening Now always in search of a new Jim Jones to lead it into an unpromised land. Nor can it mute its unswerving trust in God without becoming a religion of fervid works which invests its trust in nothing but obsessive activity.

This faith cannot give up its fierce passion without slipping into a passivity laced with the sort of "niceness" one sees in the befuddled grin on the face of a cartoon character. The nature of Christian faith cannot rest on such mindless foundations, for these play no authentic role as aspects of that faith which drive it to act. Today's lessons leave no doubt that such caricatures of faith will not only hamstring the faith but fall beneath God's judgment.

The Fourth Sunday after Pentecost

Lutheran	Roman Catholic	Episcopal	Pres/UCC/Chr	Meth/COCU
Exod. 19:2–8a	Exod. 19:2–6	Exod. 19:2–8a	Exod. 19:2–6	Exod. 19:2–8a
Rom. 5:6–11	Rom. 5:6–11	Rom. 5:6–11	Rom. 5:6–11	Rom. 5:6–11
Matt. 9:35—10:8	Matt. 9:36—10:8	Matt. 9:35—10:8 (9–15)	Matt. 9:36—10:8	Matt. 9:35—10:15

EXEGESIS

First Lesson: Exod. 19:2–8a. The strand of Elohist traditions associated with the northern kingdom in the eighth and ninth centuries B.C. persistently reflects a concern for the separateness and exclusivity of Israel's faith and practice. This passage appears to belong to that strand, presenting Israel's distinctive obligations in the form of a historical prologue to the covenant made between God and the people. Yet whatever its exact date, its covenant renewal pattern invites resignification in subsequent generations. During an era when the cultic, political, and social temptations toward syncretism and accommodation of local religious traditions were intense, this text would have offered a powerful corrective, almost like a pageant of Israel's origins in the wilderness.

The figure of Moses functions in the role of messenger between God and the people. His shuttle diplomacy establishes the terms between this people that has been led out of Egypt into the wilderness to this encampment before the mountain of God and God who has brought them to himself. All the initiative lies with God, and the story indicates clearly that this is not a conditional agreement between equal partners. The people and their elders are only able to consent or reject, and with all that God has already done, they all answer together agreeing that "all that the Lord has spoken we will do."

The conditional element of 19:5 is limited to the continued reception of the blessings promised for a people chosen to be a kingdom of priests and a holy nation among all peoples. Thus the brunt of the story is directed at a later generation and its identity. God has already redeemed Israel from Egypt, cut a covenant with the people, and established them in a distinctive vocation in the land as promised. All the people have already accepted the terms of God's treaty with them. But now it is incumbent upon subsequent generations to maintain their identity as a people called out, set apart, and sanctified as belonging to God alone. The continued assurance of Israel's blessings depends on their exclusive obedience to the God who has claimed them as his exclusive possession.

Second Lesson: Rom. 5:6–11. Paul's diagnosis of the sinful human condition is uncompromising and confrontational. Long before his arguments concerning good order in the church and obedience to civil authorities were perceived by many as threats to various efforts at social reform and liberation, his portrayal of humanity prior to Christ as without strength and in bondage to sin evoked a host of objections from philosophical, ethical, and religious defenders of human integrity and virtue. He will not even allow that a few exemplary saints, sages, or heroes could attain perfection and serve as exemplars and patrons for the rest of humanity. Yet is it not his purpose to wallow in a doctrine of total depravity or to demean all human cultural virtue and achievement in order to magnify God. The diagnosis is much more specific to his theological and soteriological argument. It cannot be lightly dismissed as the world-denying fantasy of a primitive first-century apocalyptic or neurotic mind.

This passage clearly shows the soteriological perspective from which his severe anthropological diagnosis is offered. It is the gospel which discloses the abject futility of all merely human efforts to justify our existence before God and the world. It is amazing grace which permits and requires us to recognize how dire our condition and how vain our efforts at self-improvement had been. Only divine intervention to the point of the sacrificial death of God's Son and Messiah, astonishing as that was, could come to terms with our condition. This is not a prideful denigration of all efforts at social and personal improvement. It is an admission by the faithful people of the external, objective, and divine source of health and salvation.

Thus Paul fairly sings with the joy of the redeemed. The magnitude of this salvation can only be estimated in wonder. "How much the more" is the hymn of those who have been justified and reconciled while still ungodly and at enmity with God. The confidence and assurance of the reconciled both furnish courage to admit the gravity of the fallen human condition and provide a glimpse of the grandeur of divine salvation which is still unfolding.

Gospel: Matt. 9:35—10:8. This section of Matthew's Gospel displays an unusual degree of the evangelist's editorial activity. It gathers up a summary of Jesus' ministry of word and deed in Israel (9:35), introduces the mission charge to his disciples as necessitated by the dire state of the people (9:36—10:4), and identifies their initial mission as targeted exclusively on these "lost sheep of the house of Israel" (10:5–8). In spite of the fact that this material appears in disparate contexts in Mark, Matthew's account holds together to provide a poignant and tragic view of the mission of the Messiah and his disciples in Israel.

The poignancy of the section arises from the image of the people as "harassed and helpless, like sheep without a shepherd," evoking Jesus' compassion and commission of his disciples (9:36–37). Without developing fine distinctions between the scribes, Pharisees, and Sadducees, Matthew has been building the case that the religious leaders of Israel are increasingly hostile to Jesus and intent on turning the people against him. While the crowds have marveled saying, "Never was anything like this ever seen in Israel," the Pharisees have passed judgment saying, "He casts out demons by the prince of demons" (9:33–34). Instead of helping the people to recognize and receive the Messiah, these religious leaders are proving to be false shepherds harassing the flock. The mission to Israel is already a desperate campaign against great odds.

The tragedy of the rejection of Jesus Messiah that will follow will not only result in the complicity of all of Israel in the Messiah's death (27:25; see 21:37–41) and the destruction of Jerusalem (22:7), but even "the kingdom of God will be taken away from you and given to a nation producing the fruits of it" (21:43). Yet no delight can be taken even by gentile interpreters. This account is written from within the fold of Israel by an evangelist who brings a prophetic indictment against his own people. The Messiah is intent on saving his lost and defiant people. The mission to the Gentiles will eventually proceed in concession of the failure of the mission to Israel. Even the disciples are sent without pretense or pride of place, like sheep among wolves (10:16). "You received *gratis,* give *gratis.*" The disciples of this Messiah who identified with Israel can never abandon the hope or the mission that all of Israel may yet receive Jesus its Messiah and his salvation.

HOMILETICAL INTERPRETATION

In the various readings which have been dealing with the community's faith since Pentecost Sunday, the notion of mission has occurred more than once. The very foundation of the faith in the person of the risen Lord is recounted by John (The Day of Pentecost) and Matthew (The Holy Trinity) in terms of a bestowal of pneumatic authority and mission to the world. These are uniquely Jesus' to give, since he himself has fulfilled his own mission as Messiah to Israel— being anointed of God by the Spirit in his baptism at John's hands, and being anointed in his own blood in his passion and death. The Anointed One's exclusive position as source for the quality and nature of the community's faith flows from this fact, being the burden of the lessons for the past two Sundays. Today's readings dwell on the mission of that faith in detail.

Once again the norm of faithful Christian mission is seen in the person of the Messiah as he fulfills his own mission in the days of his flesh. Matthew depicts him going about all the cities and towns, *teaching* in synagogues, *preaching* the good news of the imminent

kingdom, and *healing* every disease and infirmity (9:35). Seeing the
people languishing untended in their needs, harassed and helpless
without a shepherd, he summons his disciples to their aid. Their
mission is to the "lost sheep of the house of Israel" (10:6), and he
sends them to do what he has been doing (10:7–8). Israel left in such a
dire condition is rejecting the Messiah of God to its own peril.

While it does not fall easily upon modern minds, Matthew makes
clear that the righting of this dangerous situation will not be accomplished, at least in Jesus' own view, by any but the most radical
means. New elections will not do. Better educational systems will not
do. The powers Jesus gives his apostolic missionaries do not include
political insight or learned competencies. He makes them exorcists
(10:1), proclaimers of the kingdom (10:7), and healers of affliction
(10:8). Later (10:16–24) he implies that sacrifice of their own liberty
and their very lives will become necessary. This turned out to be the
case for both him and them.

These powers and results of mission are symptoms of how deeply
Jesus diagnosed the obstacles confronting him and his followers. The
obstacles are not at root human inadvertences which mute human
goodwill. The powers he gives his missionaries are far too radical to
suggest this. The price he and they will have to pay belies this. His
diagnosis is uncompromising and confrontational: it is of the human
condition itself steeped in sin. It is this which must be lanced at the
deepest level. The world cannot merely be modified: it must be
recreated, and only the Messiah's sacrificial death can accomplish
this in God's charity (Rom. 5:6–11).

It is not surprising that many of Jesus' followers could not or would
not understand this. It was hard enough for them as Jews to accept the
fact that in Jesus the Word had taken flesh. It was even more an
assault on their conventional wisdoms that this same Jesus should
have died the way he did. NT reflections on this double difficulty
betray a certain slowness in coming to terms with it. But it is significant that far from softening its sharp edges or explaining it away,
those reflections eventually put the double scandal of a divine incarnation and sacrificial death at the very core of Christian faith and
mission. Historic Christian worship systems stand as effective witnesses to this fact. Baptism splices one into this faith and mission by

plunging one into his death, and at the center of every eucharistic table stands the food which nourishes that same faith and mission: his body broken, his blood poured out for the life of the world.

In view of all this, it is difficult to understand how Christians can blind themselves to what they have become in Christ. Far from being the best support of the world's status quo, Christianity is the world's exorcist, because it sees the world's possession in terms of the vengeance it wreaked on Christ. Christianity is the world's healer because it can see in Christ that the world's illness really is terminal.

But even this is to say little. The unique focus on Christ of Christian faith and mission must inevitably take us all away from conventional reassurance, the sunny platitudes of optimism, the exhilaration of glands and works and the comforts of culture. It takes us instead into regions of pain, ambiguity, and tragic distress. Our Christian celebrations, unlike those of this world, are pervaded with a millennial chill, for at the center of them all is the death of the Lover of humankind, a wounded presence which tells us more about ourselves than we want to know. It tells me that left to myself I am not really very nice: I am hard, alone, stoic at best, a killer. This is what I am if I work hard at it. If I do not work hard at it, I am merely a mindless recipient of creation's meaning-laden bounty and a leech on the labor of others like myself.

Neither alternative corresponds to sporadic yearnings in my soul. These yearnings must remain unrequited and become blunted unless I find access to the death of the Lover of humankind, to the blood of him who has trampled death by his death in that central place where the world is constantly being reborn. Works and good intentions will not take me there. Only faith in the Anointed One of God who has now become life-giving Spirit will take me there. And to this faith I come regularly only by the loving exorcism, the care-filled preaching and the tender healing which together constitute Christ's mission committed to the community of faith in him. What I have received freely, I must in turn give freely to Jew and Gentile, male and female, slave and free, to all alike in God's fierce charity. This is the heart of the community's faithful mission in him, by him, and through him who orders our affairs not from throne or office but from his cross.

The Fifth Sunday after Pentecost

Lutheran	Roman Catholic	Episcopal	Pres/UCC/Chr	Meth/COCU
Jer. 20:7–13	Jer. 20:10–13	Jer. 20:7–13	Jer. 20:10–13	Jer. 20:7–13
Rom. 5:12–15	Rom. 5:12–15	Rom. 5:15b–19	Rom. 5:12–15	Rom. 5:12–21
Matt. 10:24–33	Matt. 10:26–33	Matt. 10:(16–23) 24–33	Matt. 10:26–33	Matt. 10:16–33

EXEGESIS

First Lesson: Jer. 20:7–13. In the brief compass of these verses, Jeremiah's lament to God runs a gamut from rage and humiliation, oppression and fatigue, to confidence and doxology. In the literary context of chap. 20, this psalm follows the public mockery and beating of the prophet and precedes the depth of his despair when he curses the day of his birth. Feeling victimized by God in his inescapable vocation to proclaim a message of judgment and doom to a hostile people, Jeremiah neither sought the prophetic role nor enjoyed contentment in its execution. Merely psychological explanations of his anguish fail to plumb the depth of his aversion and compulsion. Any who would suggest that the vocation of those who are to speak for God will be a pleasant and comfortable profession would do well to come to terms with Jeremiah's laments.

Jeremiah's struggles with God are more than autobiographical glimpses. They are also reflections of the pathos of God in dealing with his people. As Jeremiah complains bitterly concerning the way he has been used and seduced into humiliation before the people, he realizes that it is as bearer of the word of the Lord that he is rejected. He knows that all the hostility and curses directed toward him are of little weight or power compared with God's intentions to accomplish his purposes in the world. He may feel deceived and overwhelmed by the magnitude of his task, but he knows that he has not been deceived so that those who hate him will overcome him (vv. 10–11). His shame, palpable and public as it is, is yet an honor compared with their great shame and enduring dishonor which will follow (v. 11).

The suffering of God's prophet is part and parcel of the working of divine justice and vengeance/vindication within history. Caught up in God's impassioned intention to confront and redirect his willful people, the prophet is fully assured of God's power both to wreak his vengeance on the unrighteous and to accomplish his saving purpose in and through his willing and unwilling agents. God's prophet and word may evoke rejection, but God will not be mocked. Even his prophet who is called to represent his justice and saving will shall yet be vindicated.

Second Lesson: Rom. 5:12–15. Sin is both the common condition of all human offspring of Adam and the shared activity of all individuals. Paul's argument cuts both ways, providing a crucial basis for the church's doctrine of original sin and provoking the awareness of the deadly consequences of the sins of all. To confess that "we are by nature sinful and unclean and that we have sinned" is fully consistent with this Pauline passage. Even if human complicity in this sinful order was not recognized or reckoned until the law made it evident and culpable, participation in this sin still worked its fatal consequences. Thus the law made this mortality all the more painful by holding humanity responsible. Death was now only "natural" to a sinful human nature.

As in the previous passage from Romans, however, it is crucial to observe that Paul moves to this stern diagnosis out of his confidence of the gift, grace, and life proffered to humanity through Jesus Christ. The beginning and end of this presentation is the vision of God's gift of grace and forgiveness. With the assurance of the surpassing potency of the grace of God, Paul dares to challenge all human efforts to deny the reality of sin, even stressing the corroborating and convicting force of the law. Only the conviction of the adequacy and efficacy of God's grace in Jesus Christ could permit such a dire reading of the human situation without resulting in despair.

Gospel: Matt. 10:24–33. Matthew's presentation of the commissioning of the disciples continues with no easy assurances. Perhaps the entire chapter should be read as a unit to grasp the scope of the warnings and promises. Particular attention should be paid to the way the charge against Jesus as being in league with the prince of demons in 9:34 is reintroduced as a warning to the disciples in 10:25. The growing rejection of Jesus by the religious leaders is clearly being used as the backdrop to interpret subsequent persecution and rejection of the church's ministry in Israel. The message is also clear: "Don't expect better treatment than your Teacher and Lord has received!"

This advance warning also conveys a profound assurance to an afflicted church. "So have no fear of them!" You have been alerted, but you also know that they do not possess the ultimate power even if they can kill. Do not be intimidated or silenced even by physical abuse and executions which disciples will undergo. With a host of aphorisms drawn from the collected sayings of Jesus, Matthew consoles and encourages the church in its contested mission.

As in Jeremiah's day, the stakes were exceedingly high. The official religious spokesmen had powers to abuse and exclude those whose word of the Lord was deemed unacceptable. The Christians did not have a "persecution complex." They were preaching a message that evoked persecution from the religious leaders who regarded Jesus as a false messiah and who resented the accusation that their rejection was sealing the dire fate of the nation. In such circumstances, only those who are assured that their witness has the authority of God and his Messiah can dare to endure hostility on behalf of their preaching. Furthermore, such believers cannot do otherwise!

HOMILETICAL INTERPRETATION

It was suggested in last Sunday's readings that the faith which gives rise to the community's mission is fraught with the same perils which dogged and eventually slew the community's Lord. This Sunday's readings are overt about these perils. It is as though Jeremiah, Paul, and Matthew conspire to teach us a hard lesson in realism.

Jeremiah himself is seen twisting and turning in God's hammerlock, desperately trying to avoid proclaiming to an already hostile people precisely what they did not want to hear. The prophet's hymn of agony at his predicament is so lyric that it could hardly fail to move any human being who has ever suffered. This is probably all a humanist could detect in the hymn. But to one of faith there is more, and the more is essential. For Jeremiah is not just *homo tragicus*. He is a prophet, one chosen either by or against his own will (it makes no difference) for a mission that extends beyond himself and stems from a source beyond himself. His fidelity to that source and his performance of his mission are all that really matter.

Prophets themselves are notoriously expendable. To one of faith, the prophet's agony is therefore not without interest, but this interest is subordinate to the prophet's transmutation of that agony into obedience to his mission and its source. It is at this point that personal agony rises to the level of saving witness to the nature of things and thus attracts the universal interest of all people. No faithful Christian can read this passage without sensing beneath its pain-wracked rhythms the agony of another prophet in a garden outside Jerusalem, one whose passionate mission Jeremiah the prophet is already beginning to reveal.

Like Jeremiah, Paul begins with pain and death and moves through obedience to saving witness graced finally by God in Christ. Two lessons stand out. First, the agony and fatality we daily discover to prey upon our lives are of our own making, and both the condition and its lethal results are to be traced not to some of us but to all. Furthermore, this condition is the fruit of personal choice rather than the impersonal workings of a flawed creation. Things or structures do not sin or choose death: people do. As smallpox was transmitted to aboriginal peoples not by ships or missionary societies or imperialism but by people bearing the virus, so we generate sin in God's good world by misuse of created things and of the structures we set up with pathetic goodwill to alleviate precisely the disease we ourselves have chosen to bear. "Sin came into the world through one man and death through sin, and so death spread to all men because all men sinned" (Rom. 5:12). This lesson is not a pretty one. But we are not a pretty folk despite our occasional bursts of glory. These echoes of our divine origin are impressive indeed, but even Bach's Mass in B Minor cannot save the world. A faithful community's mission is therefore not to the arts, or to culture or structures or causes, no matter how good these may be. It is to us, for we are the problem.

The second tough lesson is that the solution to the problem is

available exclusively in Jesus Christ. He graces Paul's dire diagnosis
of the human situation, saving that diagnosis from mere pessimism or
despairing stoicism. Despite the fact that our condition has been
terminal since we fell by choice, the divine physician undertook its
cure (not merely its alleviation) from its very inception. Our story
since then has been a history of salvation in which even the expulsion
from Eden, the imposition of the law, and periodic chastisements
even of God's chosen people are to be seen as remedies patiently
advancing the restoration of our lives. Classic Christianity has always
made remembrance (anamnesis) of this history the central factor in its
preaching and Eucharist, seeing it as the only frame within which the
past presence of Jesus Christ in the flesh, and his continuing real
presence by faith and grace in his church, make sense. Since God's
healing of our condition began with our first sin and continues down
into the specifics of every generation's present, anamnesis can never
be mere ecclesiastical nostalgia. Anamnesis remembers precisely by
confessing the presence of God's consummate cure of our condition
in Christ here and now—in the Word heard and preached, in the
sacrament of the Word faithfully observed and celebrated.

Yet none of this adds up to a prescription for Christians to drift off
into the mindless euphoria of unwarranted optimism. Matthew points
out in today's Gospel that salvation neither past nor present is cheap
or easy. This history of that salvation is told over and over again, lest
we forget. That story, which is good news indeed, pivots on the death
of a man who is Lord. Thus no faithful preaching of that gospel and no
faithful enactment of it in any sacrament can pivot upon anything less.
Matthew cautions Christians in every age, "Don't expect better
treatment than your teacher and Lord received." But he also insists
that Christians should have no fear of those who treat them ill, since
the most they can do is kill, and the Lord has overcome death.

This gives rise to the rich paradox that lies at the core of all
Christian endeavor. It is given most stunning expression when Christians assemble on the Lord's Day. What they have claimed to do there
for two thousand years is to celebrate the death of the Lord whose
true day is the whole of time itself. They do this by being faithful to his
command that they "do this" as his anamnesis until he comes in the
glory that is his by right of conquest. For he has carried off the spoils

of the death we ourselves loose in the world of his own fashioning, destroying that death by his death. In him we are made whole, though we twist and turn in earthly agony like Jeremiah, Paul, and even the Lord himself. It is good that we should be here, for this place makes us not nostalgic, pessimistic, or stoic. It makes us, rather, what the world cannot be without and survive its sin: clear-eyed realists who rejoice in his triumph by reigning with him from his cross. For here alone is the world not merely comforted but cured, being reborn fresh and new.

The Sixth Sunday after Pentecost

3rd

Lutheran	Roman Catholic	Episcopal	Pres/UCC/Chr	Meth/COCU
Jer. 28:5–9	2 Kings 4:8–11, 14–16a	Isa. 2:10–17	2 Kings 4:8–16	2 Kings 4:8–16
Rom. 6:1b–11	Rom. 6:3–4, 8–11	Rom. 6:3–11	Rom. 6:1–11	Rom. 6:1–11
Matt. 10:34–42	Matt. 10:37–42	Matt. 10:34–42	Matt. 10:37–42	Matt. 10:34–42

EXEGESIS

First Lesson: 2 Kings 4:8–16. This pericope appears to have been lifted from its context in order to illustrate the receiving of a prophet's reward for receiving a prophet as mentioned in the Gospel (Matt. 10:41). Indeed it is a good example of Semitic hospitality being extended to a "holy man of God," and the woman was presented as innocent of manipulation. Her gracious reception of the prophet does not look for reward, and even her confidence in the prophet's promise of a child is filled with apprehension. She did not intend to put the prophet or God to any test. Yet the story is truncated by stopping at v. 16. Not only is the immediate conclusion concerning the conception and birth of the promised son thereby cut off, but the crucial episode that concludes this elaborate story is missing. The ensuing death and revivification of the son of the Shunammite woman both test and vindicate her unshaken confidence in the prophet and holy man who is the mediator of God's saving power.

The story introduces the reader to the ancient lore surrounding the legendary figures of Elijah and Elisha. The strange and marvelous stories of Elisha's powers echo the traditions of Elijah and will serve as precedents for the miracles of the prophet Jesus (see especially 1 Kings 17:17–24; Luke 7:11–17), and this section of 2 Kings (4:1— 8:6) is filled with a series of wonder stories, concluding with yet another restoration to this Shunammite woman. First her son is restored and then her house and her land (see 8:1–6). Even the word spoken on her behalf to the king or commander of the army which she first declined is later accomplished by Elisha's servant (4:13; 8:1–6).

The exact political associations of this story are now quite obscure. The strategic location of Shunem near Samaria between north and south may at one time have been crucial to its impact as a demonstration of the power and beneficence which the prophet possessed even in border regions. Some of these stories from the Elijah and Elisha cycles may even seem to be only hagiographic legends without much theological content. Yet as the traditional maxim of Matt. 10:41 and the larger context of 2 Kings indicate, hospitality extended toward God's prophets and apostles was regarded with awe as full of promise. This entire narrative would probably have been well-known in popular tradition surrounding a "prophet" with the hopes and fears of those who behold the power of God.

Second Lesson: Rom. 6:1–11. Paul's radical analysis of human bondage to sin and death and of the liberation from that bondage through Christ sharpens the ethical question. Freedom from the power and domination of sin and death does not require the flaunting of sin or give license to sinful behavior by a spiritual elite. Such an interpretation, which is often the obverse of a world-denying asceticism, would only represent a new bondage, an alternative form of living "according to" the dictates of the twisted order that has prevailed so long. A new logic of grace must be substituted as the basis of the Christian life.

In a magnificent appeal to baptismal death and regeneration, Paul emphasizes that Christian freedom from sin and death has been effected through death, that is, first of all through the objective and prior death of Christ Jesus, and through the Christian's incorporation into that death in Baptism. The tenses of the passage reflect a careful schema by which the precedence of what has happened to Christ in death and resurrection producing his current exaltation is objectively established as the basis for what has been accomplished, what is the present possibility, and what is the future promise in the life of the Christian. The scenario is not yet complete for the believer, although Christ has completed his course. Thus the present life of the Christian has been dramatically altered by the fact of participation through Baptism in Christ's death. Not only does that have eschatological consequences for life *with* Christ through resurrection, but it means that those incorporated *in* his conquest of sin and death in his death have themselves been freed from sin (v. 7). The possibility of walking in newness of life has been granted to those who have died with Christ in the burial of Baptism.

The ethical goal of the argument must not, however, be overlooked. The issue is the Christian life, and all the force of Paul's objective evangelical theology is brought to bear on an appeal for a perspective as to what has been put to death and what constitutes the new life. Christian freedom is preoccupied not with sin but with God. The new bondage to righteousness through incorporation into Christ is finally a freedom that does not require displays of indifference to sin. Rather it enables hope for the life disposed toward God (see 6:20–23).

Gospel: Matt. 10:34–42. Christian discipleship continues to be the subject of this section of the Gospel, and the uncompromising requirements of following Jesus cannot be evaded. Yet the probable historical setting of Matthew's account prevents reading these words as a sectarian and masochistic salvation through suffering. They are rather a pastoral assurance and realistic warning to a beleaguered community.

The shared expectation of the messianic age as an era of peace is well represented in the NT and diverse contemporary Jewish writings, but the prophetic heritage also testifies to the fact that divine intervention and participation in human history has the effect of convulsing the world. Far from offering a benediction on the status quo, the reign of God and his Messiah presents a threat to existing orders, and the prophet or disciples would be well advised to know that. The very alienations and interpersonal hostilities that the prophet Micah (7:6) had diagnosed in his time are further disclosed and magnified by the actual appearance of the Messiah. The peace and salvation which the Messiah offers will rarely be evident within existing human institutions and relationships.

In a context where confessing Jesus as Messiah and Lord often meant exclusion from family and community or even loss of social opportunity and persecution, Matthew's collection of Jesus' warnings would serve to comfort and encourage faithfulness. This is not a general attack on family ties but an appeal to the true source of peace and security and lasting relationships in the face of competing loyalties. Perhaps only those Christians who have confronted similar tests of their confession in overtly hostile surroundings can best bear witness to the consolation of this passage.

Yet the concluding verses also display the evangelist's goal in the recitation of such severe warnings. The assurance of divine involvement in the mission of the Messiah and his disciples contains the promise of the "prophet's reward" and the "righteous man's reward." Both the prophet and the righteous man were known as frequent victims of hostility and injustice, but God's participation in their cause guaranteed their vindication. So also even those who befriended the disciples of Jesus could be confident of sharing in this eschatological reward.

HOMILETICAL INTERPRETATION

The fascinating thing about today's three readings is the way in which they build a fugue on the mode or style the community's faith is expected to take.

In view of the candid exposure last Sunday's lessons gave to the perils attending the community's faith, today's lessons are filled with the dialectical response of pastoral assurance, hope, eschatological peace, and a certain consolation for the beleaguered. While it is true that these are typically "messianic" themes as distinguished from the

more "prophetic" themes of judgment, chastisement, and convulsion
which attend God's intervention in the world, the two sets of themes
cannot be allowed to drift apart in such a way that the community
might feel free to opt for one set or the other according to its own
preference. That this happens may be seen in the perception by many
people of Christianity as a religion of consolation which works by
finding only the kindest words of the gentle Jesus to apply to those
who seek comfort in the stress of daily living. Fewer people today
seem to regard Christianity as a prophetic enterprise calling all to
judgment and repentance.

The point to be made, however, is that while reductionism may
throw light briefly on one facet of reality, it warps the whole. Our
modern tendency to prefer and preach mostly messianic themes of
assurance, hope, peace, and consolation risks warping the gospel. It
assures our deafness to the subtle interweaving of messianic and
prophetic themes in today's readings. The Son of man comes bringing
not peace but a sword; yet he embraces children, is moved to mercy
on the death of Lazarus, and weeps over his people and their city.
Nowhere can it be seen more clearly than in today's readings that
these apparently contradictory attitudes are not merely juxtaposed
but intimately related by being rooted in reality.

The story of the Shunammite woman from 2 Kings is a case in point.
She received the prophet with courteous liberality, waiting on him
and his servant with a frank confidence that gives serenity to her
image in this tale. As a result, the prophet untwisted her life first by
giving her the son she never had and then by giving him back to her
when the child died. The end of the story is consolation, but that
consolation for a beleaguered woman was won only by the holy man's
grappling with a twisted order of things, where limitation and death
rule with contemptuous caprice. By receiving the prophet, the
Shunammite woman received the reward that lay only in a prophet's gift.

Matthew recounts that Jesus took this fact and expanded it profoundly in his charge to those he sent out "as sheep among wolves"
(Matt. 10:16). What is in their gift to those who will receive them is not
merely a prophet's reward: it is Jesus himself and the One who sent
him. "He who receives you receives me, and he who receives me

receives him who sent me" (Matt. 10:40). No greater messianic consolation than this, coming from One who was already announcing himself as the Messiah or *Christos* of God, could be imagined. Yet this consolation can never lead to passive complacency: its roses have thorns, its peace is sharp-edged, its Messiah is a prophet who will meet on Calvary a fate like the prophet's death between sanctuary and altar. To receive him in those whom he sends is therefore to have dwelling in one's house the eye of the very hurricane which convulses the world. Here alone will one find peace—not with the world, but with the One whose Messiah sends those whom we are always to receive into our inmost midst. Jesus the Christ came in the flesh to set us at war with the world we have made for ourselves. He came in the flesh, and comes still in word and sacrament, to put us at peace with the Source of that world.

This is a hard saying, which lies at the very core of the gospel. So central is it that even if it sets child against parent and families against themselves, so must it be. Paul describes this from an individual's subjective viewpoint, both sharpening the ethical implications of the hard saying and then broadening the saying so as to encompass the whole style or mode by which communities of Christians are to live. So implacable must be one's state of war with this world that one must both be and appear to be dead to that world. This means that one must be not merely liberated from such a world but radically freed of it. The martyr knows that liberation and freedom are vastly different levels of existence, for a slave may be liberated from slavery while remaining in thrall to it. Others may liberate one, but one must free oneself. To do this one must die to what one has been. Dying brooks neither negotiation nor compromise. For this reason dying is the only perfectly revolutionary act available to any human being. Political systems therefore resist revolution against themselves just as organisms resist death to themselves, each for the same reason. And it may be the final irony of this world that the greater their resistance, the more states or individuals become enslaved to their own demise, thus precipitating by compulsion precisely what they sought to hold at bay. Death is the sick and tragic bottom line of a twisted order.

The only alternative is to choose death freely, celebrate it with flair, and then embrace its consequences with clear eye and level head.

This sort of death takes its place among the rest of God's good creatures as a creative act, betraying its Creator for the life of the world. *This* sort of death tramples that other sort of death as Christ trampled death by his death. From *this* sort of death proceeds nothing but life, the life of a new order of things restored in him whom the Father sent for no other reason than this. *This* sort of death is the vocation of all who would live in him, a life begun in turning completely away from another world and plunging into the watery tomb of Baptism into Christ's own baptism unto death. One discovers that the tomb is a womb from which issues a life never before seen on earth except in the risen Lord. It is a life in the most intimate union with the Source of life itself, with the One who sent the Son who sends those whom we receive in peace.

To live in this way is the style or mode the gospel expects the community's faith to take. This means a Christian community is a baptized and a baptizing assembly.

The Seventh Sunday after Pentecost

(handwritten: 4th)

Lutheran	Roman Catholic	Episcopal	Pres/UCC/Chr	Meth/COCU
Zech. 9:9–12	Zech. 9:9–10	Zech 9:9–12	Zech. 9:9–13	Zech. 9:9–13
Rom. 7:15–25a	Rom. 8:9, 11–13	Rom. 7:21—8:6	Rom. 8:6–11	Rom. 7:15—8:13
Matt. 11:25–30	Matt. 11:25–30	Matt. 11:25–30	Matt. 11:25–30	Matt. 11:25–30

EXEGESIS

First Lesson: Zech. 9:9–12. Dating the oracles of Zechariah 9—14 is fraught with controversy. The historical references have suggested political contexts as early as the destruction in the sixth century B.C. to as late as the second century B.C. (the time of the Maccabees). Efforts to write the history of prophetic tradition have noted the recrudescence of very primitive images of Yahweh the warrior God in literary material that is clearly later than the era of the classical

historical prophets. In fact, this very revival of ancient images of
cosmic struggle and warfare (see Exod. 15) may be the critical mark of
this prophetic material. In a time when a theodicy or a demonstration
of God's righteous involvement in history may have become ex-
tremely problematic, testimony to divine triumph above and at the
culmination of history has become the primary prophetic message.

The vision of this chapter is that of the ultimate triumph of Yahweh
with the glorious establishment of his gracious reign of peace. It is a
word to the oppressed who have seen the dreams and promises of the
kingdoms of David and Josiah fall short of the ideal and crumble. It is
a renewal of divine assurance to the captives and "prisoners of hope"
whose confidence in divine justice within history has been shaken.
The promise is eschatological, perhaps even apocalyptic: Yahweh's
own triumph will not fail.

The pericope under consideration, however, prevents the total
abandonment of a historical framework. Perhaps no specific king
could attain to this ideal, but the human regent is also celebrated in the
midst of the praises of the reign of Yahweh. The "humiliation" or
"submission" or "obedience" of this king, however, is that which
distinguishes him. Rather than simply magnifying the virtue and
beneficence of the ideal ruler, Zechariah 9 heralds the advent of a
ruler whose entire reign will be transparent to the dominion of
Yahweh himself. Israel's hope for peace and restoration lies not in the
establishment of yet another glorious or even humble king but in the
coming of the reign of Yahweh through a king whose entire demeanor
manifests his dependence on a faithful God.

Second Lesson: Rom. 7:15–25a. Few passages have generated
such exegetical and theological debate in recent years as has this text.
Long read as a cry of despair against the inner turmoil of conscience
produced by the law, Romans 7 has reinforced Christian insistence
that all legalisms of ethics, religion, and institutions are finally dis-
placed by the gospel. And indeed that insistence has proven to be of
great consequence for the release of troubled souls from the anguish
of self-condemnation.

But Paul's problem may have been much more specific to his
first-century Jewish and gentile Christian context. It must not be

overlooked that he is vigorous in his defense of the validity of the law in this section and that he is about to launch into an elaborate discussion of the relation of gentile Christianity to Christian and non-Christian Israel (Romans 9—11). The problem of the Torah and its validity now that the Messiah has come is a lively pastoral and community issue which requires interpretation.

The virtue of the law is twofold: it displays what is right, to which the healthy mind and conscience give ready and eager assent, and it exposes the grave discrepancy between that which is acknowledged as right and that which is done. In rabbinic anthropology, the good inclination within the person is actually capable of recognizing what is right, but the evil inclination so dominates human actions in a sinful world that the bondage to sin is most obvious to those who know the Torah. Some moral improvement may be possible, yet no amount of faithful observance can eradicate the perversion of good intentions that actual behavior displays. The law is not adequate to liberate humanity from the sinful effects of the most enlightened intentions.

The grace of God which is potently at work in Christ Jesus provides the only remedy and liberation from the dire consequences of this discrepancy. Knowledge of the law and a robust conscience might lead only to a quietism were it not for the atoning power of Christ. The Christian also will often see sincere evangelical words, actions, and programs perverted into evil ends. But with eyes wide open to such realities, reliance upon God's grace at work through Christ enables Christians to proceed, confident of the Holy Spirit's redemption and transformation of human actions (see Rom. 8:1–11).

Gospel: Matt. 11:25–30. The severe warnings concerning the cost of Christian discipleship in the previous Pentecost texts stand in marked contrast with the gentle words of assurance in this passage. Having concluded those instructions to the twelve disciples (11:1), Matthew next presented Jesus in the context of the criticism and obduracy of the people and cities of "this generation," emphasizing the dire judgment that is in store for them (11:2–24). Recognizing the gravity of those oracles of warning and condemnation permits the interpreter to identify the peculiar content of these words of consolation.

The three sayings gathered together by the evangelist in this context permit no human pretension on God or superiority over against those who have been judged. Divine freedom of election is amply displayed in the unlikely assemblage of "babes" to whom God has disclosed his gracious purpose. Jesus is himself the bearer and revealer of God's election, and the mystery of the ignorance of the "wise and understanding" baffles human understanding (see Isa. 29:14; Pss. 8:2; 19:7; 1 Cor. 1:19). The yoke of Jesus' instruction is not the burden of the Lord or of the obligation of great learning in the law. Jesus' thanksgiving to God at the obscurity of his teaching to the high and mighty rather emphasizes the pure gift that it offers to those who are innocent of learning. Not that study of the law was thereby denigrated, but the overwhelming conviction of the absolute human dependence on God was thereby displayed. Nothing qualifies humanity to learn or receive this instruction. Claims of special status are dismissed. Only God's gracious disposition through Christ makes his self-disclosure available to humanity.

HOMILETICAL INTERPRETATION

This Sunday's lessons address the question of what sort of confidence the community's faith bears.

Most obvious is the fact that all three lessons root the faithful community's confidence squarely in the irresistible will of God and its gifts. God will have his way, no matter how obscure his will may appear, no matter how protracted its working out may seem to the community in any one era. Nor does God leave the community meantime in the lurch. No matter how invincible the will of creation's Sovereign, it is at the same time gentle, caring, and supportive as it works in time and space. The faithful community is never merely "effected" as the passive recipient of God's causal will: it is constantly "affected" by that same will, gifted at every step in its historic unfolding. What the Creator begets he also nourishes and continually holds in being, for this too is his sovereign will. As the whole of creation is not merely the effect of the Creator's will but the subject of its fulfillment, so the faithful community is both offspring and spouse of its Lord and Master—not only his issue but his lover. Unequal though the two may be, together they concelebrate a common will, their inequality itself demonstrating the free generosity of both the will and its dynamic gifts of faith, hope, and fierce charity.

The splendor of this gracious disposition throws into stark outline those areas in which the faithful community simply cannot invest its confidence, no matter how tempting these may appear as short-term refuges.

Zechariah cautions Israel about placing its weary confidence in temporal rulers. It is not that such rulers may turn out to be fickle or even wicked. Zechariah puts a harder case. Even when temporal rulers, temporal structures, temporal programs are in fact good, they still do not qualify as opportunities for the community's investment of absolute confidence. At best they are occasions for the community to sense anew the working out of the divine will which transcends even the best this world can offer. "If this king be good," Zechariah seems to say, "how much better will be that ruler whose entire being bespeaks his unqualified dependence upon God's sovereign will? Praise good rule and give thanks for the rest in tribulation it provides. But do not forget that God's will rules it even as it rules you. Here you have no abiding sovereign."

In like manner, Paul cautions Jewish Christians about placing absolute confidence even in the law. The most reverent and meticulous observance of the law's imperatives does not liberate definitively from sin. More often it leads with weary regularity to obsession, complacency, or at best to a sort of learned quietism. "The law is not identifiable with God's will," Paul seems to say. "It is only one temporary gift of that will, a will which has now manifested itself consummately in the reality of God in Christ. The law has given way to the Word made flesh, who has taken for himself a new people who are his body."

The upshot of Paul's teaching is that the faithful community does not invest its confidence in some future manifestation of God's will. In Christ that will has shone forth definitively and remains abroad in the community's midst as a living, judging, and nourishing presence. The faithful community's confidence is therefore built in, and it is based wholly on Christ.

The lesson from Matthew details what this means. First, the confidence of the faithful community does not sink its roots into a nostalgic knowledge, often romanticized, of the historical Jesus. To know him is to know the Father, who is the Source of all things and Lover of humankind. Jesus is less the baffle to knowledge of this giddy truth than he is the singular and awesome threshold to such knowledge. To look into the eyes of the *Christos* is to gaze straight into creation's center and into the love by which all other loves are named. If the law veiled this with the reverence of legal ordinances and stipulations in order to protect our frailty, the incarnation of the Word tore the veil away at last. It revealed God's fierce charity and justice for what they always had been: a love and an implacable rectitude of One who was not beyond weeping for a friend or taking children onto his lap or dying on a cross for love of all. The I Am who terrified Moses, drove prophets into frenzy, chastised the chosen people, and dumbfounded scholars of the law has entered our house and sat down to dinner.

Second, the confidence of the faithful community is the kind that binds friends together. It is no longer the kind that binds lawgiver and subject together. The faithful community's confidence is not the sort that comes with attaining a Ph.D., but that which binds child to parent and parent to child. It is not an intellectual confidence that may condescend to express itself through the senses. It is a sensual confidence that may emerge on the intellectual level, there to confound those of merely mental agility. This sort of confidence finds it wise to die for one's child or to love one's enemy but unwise to die for one's chickens or to love a superhighway.

Third, the confidence of the faithful community comes easily and with a joy that is always surprising, since it rests upon a relationship whose burden is light and whose yoke is sweet. There is nothing sour, arcane, or heavy about coming home, nor must one take a course in homecoming in order to laugh at the sight of beloved faces. Christians laugh at death because the Lover of humankind has so trampled it as to have made its lugubrious pretensions comic in their eyes—the court jester of creation rather than its premier demagogue. Christians dance with creation in all its aspects, for the Lover of all has exorcised it of the goblins we ourselves invented and then infested it with. Christians feast with splendor, and with constant pity, at a cosmic table on which the Creator of all has become food along with the humblest creature that ever yielded up its life that others might live.

The faithful community's confidence is robust, built in, and based on Christ. It relativizes nothing but the irrelevant.

The ~~Eighth~~ Sunday after Pentecost

5th (handwritten above "Eighth")

Lutheran	Roman Catholic	Episcopal	Pres/UCC/Chr	Meth/COCU
Isa. 55:10–11	Isa. 55:10–11	Isa. 55:1–5, 10–13	Isa. 55:10–13	Isa. 55:1–5, 10–13
Rom. 8:18–25	Rom. 8:18–23	Rom. 8:9–17	Rom. 8:12–17	Rom. 8:18–25
Matt. 13:1–9 (18–23)	Matt. 13:1–23 or Matt. 13:1–9	Matt. 13:1–9, 18–23	Matt. 13:1–17	Matt. 13:1–23

EXEGESIS

First Lesson: Isa. 55:1–5, 10–13. The epilogue of Isaiah 40—55 echoes the refrain of the prologue (40:6ff.). To a people who have experienced the defeat of the theocratic monarchy and the extended triumph of heathen empires in the context of their exile from the land promised to them by God, this book of the consolation of Israel begins and ends with the affirmation of the constancy of God's word. The transience of all life and human institutions ("All flesh is grass. . . . surely the people is grass," 40:6–7) has been thoroughly obvious to oppressed Israel. The power of God to deliver on his covenants with the nation has been much less clear. For the faithful, the alternative to skepticism, cynicism, or despair may have been only the contemplation of the inscrutable mystery of God's purposes and methods: "My thoughts are not your thoughts. . . . my ways are higher than your ways" (55:8–9).

The efficacy of God's word constitutes the ground for the promise of Israel's return that is restated yet again in the verses that follow (12–13). This is not a magical view of the word as an independent hypostasis or divine agency. It is an affirmation of the articulate and indeflectible will of God which shall have its way within history. This assertion corresponds closely to many other scriptural statements of warning and assurance, perhaps especially to Jeremiah's view of the compelling force of God's word and will.

The agricultural images are particularly appropriate both for reminding the reader of human dependence on God for the means of life itself and for conveying the image of the vulnerability and productivity of God's word when it is broadcast in human history. Exactly *how* or *when* it will yield its fruit is not rigidly determined, but *that* the harvest will come is sure. The vicissitudes of contexts and conditions will have an effect. But as surely as the showers provoke and produce growth and harvest on earth, so shall God's promise not fail of fulfillment.

Second Lesson: Rom. 8:18–25. Having wrestled at length with a careful interpretation of the goodness of the law, Paul has returned to his presentations of God's redemptive accomplishment of the requirement of the law. The eschatological consequences of that divine action have been fully assured to those who have been inspired to trust in Christ, and even the present existence of believers has been described as full of hope and freedom. Nevertheless no easy spiritual escapes are offered from the problems, sufferings, and struggles that afflict all who live in the present order.

The subjection of the entire creation to futility and decay is a doctrine of cosmic proportion and apocalyptic consequence. Like many other Jewish interpreters of the exilic and postexilic periods, Paul sees the drama of salvation in larger than human historical dimensions. Creation and redemption, beginning and eschaton, first and second Adam are bound together in the divine economy. Even those who have now glimpsed and grasped God's decisive redemptive intervention on behalf of his people and world still must await the ultimate consummation of history. The vocation of the believer remains to witness and serve within this world.

Hope, however, is the distinctive mark of the Christian life, and this hope has all the content of the faith that has been manifested in Christ and bestowed on the believer. The consummation of time and ultimate redemption of the whole world remains to be seen, but Paul is not advocating blind hope or exhorting hope against hope. Indeed it is in and through hope that God has exercised his dominion within a creation that was unwillingly dominated by futility. The antidote to fatalism, which was so common in the first-century world, was no simple program of self-assertion or human liberation. Rather the ground for trust in God and hope in God's future was provided by the conviction that divine involvement and participation in the suffering and death in Christ had already been vindicated by resurrection. Christian patience for God to complete this redemption throughout all of creation, including the bodily existence of the believers, was thus filled with hopeful expectation.

Gospel: Matt. 13:1–9. The parable of the sower (13:18) must be read in its entirety (vv. 1–23) and in close comparison with Mark's version if the distinctive emphases of the evangelists are to be grasped. Although his abiding interest in the christological debates surrounding the person and work of Jesus can never be ignored, Matthew's presentation of Jesus' parable draws the reader's attention more to the diversity of receptions of the Word (that is, to the different types of soil) than to the identity of the sower or content of the Word. Perhaps by reading his version backward from the allegorical application of the parable (vv. 18–23) Matthew's didactic understanding of the parable itself can be more clearly recognized. As the introduction to the parable chapter in Matthew, this passage also marks a significant turning point in the teaching of the Messiah within Israel. The mixed and often adverse reactions to Jesus' teaching have affected even the presentation of the parable itself.

The grand and surprising yield in Mark's version where "thirtyfold and sixtyfold and a hundredfold" are produced in spite of all the obstacles (Mark 4:8) now has been less dramatically perceived by the reversal of the order of the numbers (Matt. 13:8) as an outstanding to modest to poor yield. Matthew's reference to the seeds also emphasizes the mixed yield rather than confronting the reader with the unexpected growth in spite of unlikely conditions. The problem of unbelief has required Jesus to speak in parables, "*because* seeing they do not see" (compare Mark, "in order that they may not see"), and Scripture is adduced to demonstrate that the prophetic word has always had the effect of further hardening the heart of unrepentant Israel. Indeed the parables are only enigmas to all but those whose eyes and ears have been gifted to see and hear (see 13:16, 34–35; Ps. 78:2).

The passage is not merely a moral homily or lesson in listening. It is an indictment of Israel, of the people of God. The problem of unreceptive people cannot be glossed over by focusing on the great yield that resulted anyway. Matthew has used this parable and others to confront and diagnose the uneven and adverse reception that Jesus' and early Christian preaching received in Israel.

HOMILETICAL INTERPRETATION

Isaiah, Paul, and Matthew today conspire to excise from the community any notion that its faith is abstract, atemporal, or the result of mere idealism. The sacred writers insist that the faith of the community is concrete, rooted in time but not relativized by time, and normative for all. The lesson these writers teach is one which the community, always beset by those who would have it become either more or less than it is, needs to relearn over and over again.

Part of the problem, as Isaiah candidly recognizes, lies in the very difference between God and humankind. We think in brief spans of time, and our expectations are geared accordingly. We live in generations, God in aeons. He does not think in our terms, for he does not "think" at all: he simply exists. He does not behave as we do: he simply acts and all things come to be in that act. His time scale knows no past or future: in him these are nothing but a constant present. While it is strictly a thought which we cannot think, the fact is that in God the consummation of all things is, and always has been, a presently accomplished reality even while to us it seems to struggle endlessly toward fulfillment. Faith and hope are thus tied to us who are time-bound. This is why God, who is not so bound, is "faithless" and "hopeless"; what we believe, God has always known; that for which we hope, God has always possessed. In the days of Isaiah's flesh and Israel's blunted patience, God's word already had passed over into glory from before always. The Godhead we revere does not "wait": It is.

God's word and will are efficacious, therefore, in both Israel and church not because God is powerful or "faithful" or even patient. His word and will are efficacious simply because they are already consummated in him. We may lurch dubiously toward this end, but God is already there—no matter what cynics, skeptics, or gnostics would have us believe. The victory is not in doubt, and its celebration has already begun.

Giddy though this realization may be, it is an inevitable conclusion for one who thinks hard about God. Pagans and other non-Christians can, and regularly have, reached the same conclusion. The realization is neat, pure, irresistible, and awesome. Pantheists use it to insist that everything must therefore be God, and in doing so they wipe out time and space. Dualists use it to insist that no thing can be God, and in doing so they render creation evil. In either case, the deity is protected, but humanity is left adrift upon a sea of amoral fatalism where nothing but manners and graceful self-destruction can rise as authentic human monuments.

Judaism with its sustained doctrine of Israel as some sort of evolutionary corporate "incarnation" of God in space and time by covenant, law, and Messiah, and Christianity with its doctrine of the church as a final corporate "incarnation" in space and time of him who emerged from Israel as its *Christos,* both belie these fatalisms. They do so by maintaining the deepest reverence for God and all his creatures—including time and space and humankind—but without divorcing these from him or confusing them with him.

Compared to this, pantheism and dualism are systems of reasonable presumptions and conclusions which often produce austerely lovely artifacts such as Shinto ritual, Zen Buddhist asceticism, Taoist aphorisms, or Catharist piety. Yet while all these lend superb discipline to the senses, they cannot cope with the seismic results which an incarnation of God in time and space must produce, especially when such an incarnation is for the end of a death-obliterating death. Risk is introduced into "perfect" systems by such an incarnation, for there is nothing neat or tidy about Israel, a crucifixion, or the church. Even the perfect teaching by God's Son was received diversely by the Israel which was his own people (Matthew).

But perhaps the most astonishing result of traditional Jewish and Christian teaching is the willingness of this tradition to "risk time." All peoples know what it is to wait for what will be in the future. But no people except Christians await the future in the past and present tenses. Isaiah and Paul recognize that history yet awaits its fulfillment. Paul waits, witnesses, and serves that end with hope. But both he and Matthew are aware that in the time of their writing the end of their hope had already begun. This absolutely rules out despair, even though pain and strife remain. They are in the end time, the eschaton; they lack only the end as it subsists eternally in God, the Parousia.

What the sacred writers say about their own situation must be said as well of the faithful community they address both then and now, for it is the same community of the same faith. They imply that the faithful community is not a "natural" community which is made holy by its works. If Christ be truly risen, and be truly rising still among his faithful ones by faith, grace, and sacrament, then they in him constitute the presence in this world of that "world which is to come," the kingdom, the new age. God's word and will are efficacious in the community, and the community is therefore efficacious in its ministry of reconciliation in the world, simply because that word, that will, that community are all consummated in Christ the Word, dead and risen.

It is for this reason that Christian tradition East and West has regarded the worshipful proclamation of that consummate Word, and the worshipful celebration of that Word in the sacraments of Baptism and Eucharist, as central to the community's existence and ministry. As the ancient eucharistic prayer of St. John Chrysostom still puts it: "You brought us from nothing into being, you raised us when we had fallen, and you did not cease to do all things until you brought us back to heaven and endowed us with the kingdom which is to come." Christian worship does not shore up a natural community with sporadic grace as needed. Christian worship is the act of a restored world celebrating its reunion with its source for the life of all. It is the faith of the community consummated in act—concrete, rooted in time, and normative for all—the pulse of a new order whose finale is already under way in heaven.

The N̶i̶n̶t̶h̶ 6th Sunday after Pentecost

Lutheran	Roman Catholic	Episcopal	Pres/UCC/Chr	Meth/COCU
Isa. 44:6–8	Wisd. 12:13, 16–19	Wisd. 12:13, 16–19	2 Sam. 7:18–22	Isa. 44:6–8 or Wisd. 12:13, 16–19
Rom. 8:26–27	Rom. 8:26–27	Rom. 8:18–25	Rom. 8:18–25	Rom. 8:26–27
Matt. 13:24–30 (36–43)	Matt. 13:24–43 or Matt. 13:24–30	Matt. 13:24–30, 36–43	Matt. 13:24–35	Matt. 13:24–43

EXEGESIS

First Lesson: Isa. 44:6–8. God himself lays down the challenge and hauls all other gods and idols into court for judgment. In a startling image of divine self-assertion, this prophetic text presents God as making his own case for his absolute ascendancy above and beyond all others: "I am the first and I am the last; besides me there is no god" (44:6). Perhaps it would be historically inaccurate to regard this claim as a statement of radical monotheism, but then the candor of the challenge is all the more sharply apparent.

Israel in exile has suffered shame and humiliation. Its confidence in the protection and power of God has been deeply shaken, but even Israel's dire experience becomes part and parcel of the vindication of God before the nations and their gods. The judgment visited upon Israel means neither the abandonment of God's promises to Israel nor his impotence to be Israel's King and Redeemer. Having settled the case with Israel (see 43:25–28), God now turns to vindicate "Jacob, my servant, Israel whom I have chosen" (44:1).

The same might and unswerving will that brought destruction to Jacob and reviling to Israel (43:28) furnishes the ground for hope. No god has proved himself so faithful to his word or so able to "announce from of old the things to come" (44:7, 8). His fixed purpose and determination identify him as the Rock (44:8; see Deut. 32). Thus the message "Fear not, nor be afraid" is no idle assurance to a captive people. God himself has put his reputation on the line, placed himself in jeopardy next to all the gods of the nations. Now Israel must also enter the case: "And you are my witnesses!" (44:8; 43:10). Before the court of world opinion, and especially before the people of Israel themselves, God has declared himself to be Israel's Judge, Redeemer, and Savior. It was he who controlled the imperial forces against Israel, and none will be able to resist his restoration of his people.

Second Lesson: Rom. 8:26–27. The necessary complement to the previous affirmations of Christian hope (8:18–25) is immediately supplied by Paul. Human proclivity toward self-concern and need of self-justification has been transcended by the direct intervention of God and continuing intercession of the Holy Spirit. Not even hope is left to stand as the adequate or necessary ground for salvation. The gospel is not merely a message about God to be grasped by the human mind and heart, but it is the announcement of God's active involvement within human lives and plans.

The theocentric vision of this passage is no threat to human identity, nor does it suggest the absorption of humanity by the overwhelming presence of God. Rather, even when human incapacity for prayer concerning the unknown future and schema of God has been faced squarely, the abiding and active presence of the Spirit assures believers that their prayers will be conformed to God's will. Relying upon this agency of the Spirit does not require mindless submission, but those who are aware of their own inability to anticipate and promote God's will and plan (see 8:28–30) are enabled to continue to hope and pray. The Holy Spirit finally supplies and warrants the content of such fervent petitions by assuring their conformity to God's purposes.

Gospel: Matt. 13:24–30. Few passages in the Gospels are so transparent to the situation of the early church as the allegorical parable of the wheat and weeds together in Matthew. In this instance, however, recent studies have shown clearly that vv. 36–43 must be treated as a separate interpretation for the church while the allegorical parable (vv. 24–30) must be regarded as conveying its own distinct meaning as directed toward the crowds (see vv. 24, 34).

Perhaps this parable once had a more simple point of comparison or contrast in Jesus' teaching, but as it stands in Matthew, every element invites allegorical identification. The master of the house is Jesus. The seed is the Word. The field is Israel (belonging to the master). The slaves are the disciples. The reapers are the angels. The enemy is the devil, and the darnel, or weeds, are those in Israel who are unfaithful or unfruitful but virtually indistinguishable from the wheat of the faithful. To be sure, the subsequent interpretation of the parable to the disciples (vv. 36–43) corroborates these identifications. Yet the parable itself serves more to interpret the present circumstance of the church in the context of a divided Israel than to stress the eschatological judgment as does the later explanation. That such final separation will eventually take place is clear (v. 30), but the parable offers a counterproposal for the way those who are receptive to Jesus' teaching and those who are not may live together in the meantime. Rather than allowing a rigid separatism, the parable advocates coexistence in expectation of the Lord's eschatological judgment.

Patience is required of the church which regards itself as faithful Israel. Its mission of fruitfulness does not require or even allow it to presume the divine prerogatives of judgment or self-vindication over against unbelieving Israel. The situation of the obdurate has been diagnosed in the most uncompromising terms, and the enigmatic parable will only confound them as it instructs the disciples. Thus, above all, the parable offers the church an interpretation and defense of its stance in the face of severe opposition from much of Israel. The temptation to sectarian exclusivism is confronted by the Lord's teaching, and the church's difficult situation of bearing witness among and within a divided people becomes its peculiar vocation.

HOMILETICAL INTERPRETATION

The lessons for this Sunday probe the peculiar nature of the community's hope. All three make it clear that this hope is *not* simply the passive awaiting of some as yet unrevealed reality to come, if it comes at all, in the future. The community is neither bereft nor ignorant of that coming reality. What is to come has already pitched its tent in the community's midst. What the community awaits is the fully worked out result of that seminal presence in the community's temporal and spatial life story. Furthermore, the community's possession, already now, of what it hopes for assures that the community itself has a cooperative role in the working out of those results in its own history. Christian hope therefore does not passively await some fabulous and unheard-of pie in the sky. In fact, what the community hopes for is what continues to generate the community itself in the here and now. What is to come is here already, working its wonders as it will—in the community, by it, and through it.

This is a freeing concept, but it is hardly novel. The farmer who does nothing but hope for the harvest is engaging in idle fantasy. He must plant the seeds, care for them, and reap. Through all this, his hope is already really present in the womb of the seed. To this presence he must dance, conforming his life and labor to its demands. At every step, the harvest for which he hopes is in process of coming to realization.

A visual metaphor of this crucial point about Christian hope may be seen in iconography. "According to the laws of optics," writes Leonid Ouspensky in *Theology of the Icon* ([Crestwood, N.Y.: St. Vladimir's Seminary Press, 1978], pp. 224–25),

> the dimensions of objects decrease with distance and the lines of perspective cross each other at the horizon. But the icon shows us the opposite. Indeed, the point of departure of its perspective is not found in the illusory depth of the image which attempts to reproduce visible space, but before the image, in the spectator himself. . . . The Seventh Ecumenical Council emphasized the perfect correspondence between the icon and the Holy Scripture, and that the icon calls us to life which the Gospel reveals. . . . In the Gospel everything is, so to speak, in inverse perspective: "The first shall be last," the meek and not the violent shall inherit the earth, and the supreme humiliation of the cross is truth, the supreme victory.

Similarly, today's lessons imply that the community's hope does not lie on the distant horizon of its future. Rather, this hope thrusts out from that flat image, coming into present and effective focus in the heart of the viewing community. The seeds of Christian hope are not thrown forward into some time of future harvest. They are implanted and germinating in the here and now, making demands on the community's life and work.

Israel bears up under its shame and humiliation, Isaiah says, not because it looks forward to God's ultimate victory over false gods and values. God has already hauled all other gods and values in to judgment and found them wanting. "I am the first and the last," says God. "I have been around, and I assure you in your travail that no other gods but I exist to place radical demands upon you. Thus, fear not nor be afraid, for your victory in me is already accomplished. Your troubles begin only when you become so distracted as to forget this fact." God does not duck Israel's troubles; in fact, Isaiah has him addressing the people precisely in their captivity. Yet such is the power of God's presence amid his suffering people that he does not merely save them *from* their tribulation: he saves them *through* it. The seed has germinated and is already exerting its demands on the community's life and work of witness to its present hope.

The same point is made by Paul. It is not the community's yearnings or good intentions which save. It is the community's fidelity by grace to God's own admixture in their lives—the *presence* in their midst of him for whom they hope—which saves. This descends even into the specifics of those concrete things for which God's Spirit enables them to pray with sure confidence and in certain conformity to his will. In this way, the unique presence of him for whom the community hopes is itself the only thing that strengthens their hope, that purifies their prayer. So far from being merely a recess for religious, ethical, aesthetic, or cultural refreshment, a faithful community's worship is nothing less than a function of the Spirit of him who is the presence of the community's hope in its midst. The Christian at worship stands on holy ground, at the center of the universe for all to see, at the beginning point from which alone flows the life of all.

Yet as Matthew shows, this is no reason for the church to become arrogant, sectarian, or holier-than-thou. Israel's tribulations and, especially, the fate in this world of God's own Son together make it impossible that the community should slip into such attitudes while remaining faithful. If there is anyone upon whom this passage from Matthew is more rough than the willfully unbelieving, it is the "believing" who have gone smug. For the presence in their midst of him for whom they hope is, in such a case, the presence of their own judgment and condemnation. If true believers stand indeed on holy ground, they stand there in fear and trembling, knowing that fear of the Lord is the beginning of wisdom. If true believers stand indeed at the center of the universe, they know that it is convertible by their sin from an Eden into a place where the grapes of God's wrath are trampled out. If true believers stand indeed at the beginning point of life, they know that they must stand there with immense patience, for not all those who will run in so special an Olympics run whole. And they stand there also with profound humility, for their presence there is an honor they can in no wise earn, and the life which flows out from there they have not made.

The community's peculiar hope is a life of obedience to the presence in its midst of him for whom it hopes, and in whom it strives for the life of the world.